TIMOTHY FINDLEY
AN ANNOTATED BIBLIOGRAPHY

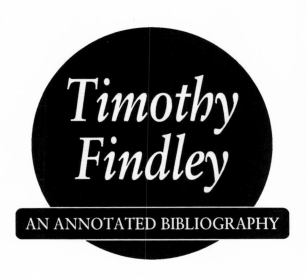

Timothy Findley

AN ANNOTATED BIBLIOGRAPHY

Carol Roberts
&
Lynne Macdonald

ECW PRESS

1990

CANADIAN CATALOGUING IN PUBLICATION DATA

Roberts, Carol
Timothy Findley: an annotated bibliography

ISBN 1-55022-112-4

1. Findley, Timothy, 1930–   — Bibliography.
2. Novelists, Canadian (English) — 20th century —
Bibliography.* 1. Macdonald, Lynne. 11. Title.

PS8511.1573Z991 1990 016.813´54 C89-094654-X
Z8296.5.R62 1990

This book has been published with the assistance of a grant from the
Canadian Federation for the Humanities, using funds provided by the
Social Sciences and Humanities Research Council of Canada.
Additional grants have been provided by the
Ontario Arts Council and The Canada Council.
Design and imaging by ECW Type & Art, Sydenham, Ontario.
Printed and bound by The Porcupine's Quill, Erin, Ontario.
Distributed by University of Toronto Press.

Published by ECW PRESS,
307 Coxwell Avenue, Toronto, Ontario M4L 3B5

TABLE OF CONTENTS

156138

INTRODUCTION

Although critical recognition has come slowly to Timothy Findley, he is now acknowledged to be one of Canada's foremost writers. As John Moss writes in *A Reader's Guide to the Canadian Novel*, "for the scope and diversity of his fiction, for the power of his prose and the precision and clarity of his vision, he is at present without peer" (C141). Findley's reputation is international and his novels have been translated into several languages. Through his work with the Writers' Union of Canada and P.E.N. International, as well as his support of other writers, he has become a respected member of both the Canadian and the international literary communities.

Timothy Findley first sought creative expression in acting, a career he pursued for several years at Canada's first Stratford Festival, in England, and the United States. He credits acting with giving his writing a sense of rhythm and cadence (C187), and critics often comment on the dramatic aspects of his work. Encouraged by actress Ruth Gordon and writer Thorton Wilder, Findley began to write seriously in 1956. During the early years of his writing career, Findley was employed by the CBC as actor, broadcaster, and scriptwriter.

His first two novels, *The Last of the Crazy People* (1967) and *The Butterfly Plague* (1969), were at first turned down by Canadian publishers and largely ignored by reviewers. *The Last of the Crazy People* was often dismissed as derivative of the Southern Gothic genre, but Findley's narrative technique, craftsmanship, and insight into a child's mind were praised in some reviews. J.M. Stedmond called Findley "a talent to keep an eye on" (D11). *The Butterfly Plague* was reviewed only twice in Canada, both times by Marian Engel (D14, D15). In one review, Engel praised Findley's good writing and his imagination, but found the novel unsatisfying (D15).

Findley's early novels and short stories reveal the themes which recur in all of his fictions as well as the vision that informs them. Findley's themes — his "obsessions" as he calls them in the Introduction to *Dinner Along the Amazon* (1984) — are violence, fascism, and war; loneliness, isolation, and the survival of the individual in a world of madness.

Several critics have pointed out the persistent use of fire and animal imagery in Findley's work. George Woodcock describes Findley's vision as an "insistence on the power of the human spirit over negation and death" (C100), while John F. Hulcoop calls it "an emphatic belief in the value of imagination" (D72). Through his work, and in interviews, Findley expresses his concern with politics, the environment, and the position of minorities in contemporary society. The writer has a responsibility, he believes, to speak out about what is wrong in society.

Critical acclaim came to Findley with publication of *The Wars* (1977) — still regarded by many as his greatest accomplishment. John F. Hulcoop writes that it "stands head and shoulders above the majority of Canadian novels" (C118). It won the Governor General's Award, an issue of *Canadian Literature* was devoted to it, and it remains the most written about of Findley's works.

Critics have discussed *The Wars*'s place in the genre of war novels, its documentary style, Findley's use of the researcher to "reconstruct" the story of Robert Ross, the authenticity of the battle scenes, and the novel's similes, images, and "crystalline" prose. The themes of isolation, violence, and the dehumanizing effect of war are often mentioned. Some critics have found in the novel naturalistic and romantic elements, seeing Ross's story as a romantic quest. Bruce Pirie calls it "a parody of romance" in which the writer uses romantic mythical forms in material of realistic content (C48). Other writers have treated this novel as an example of postmodern metafiction in which the writer plays with the conventions of fiction writing and history and is concerned with the limitations of language and visual perception. Discussion of the reader's involvement in the text is related to this critical approach. Laurie Ricou writes that the novel is not primarily the story of Robert Ross, but the extension of that story into the story of the narrator, and into the "storymaking of the reader" (C38). In another postmodernist response, Linda Hutcheon explores the problematic nature of photographs that both record and "automatize" experience (C73).

As in *The Wars*, Findley combined fact and fiction, history and invention in *Famous Last Words* (1981). This novel is Findley's most detailed examination of the theme of fascism. In discussing the novel, many critics have concentrated on Findley's technique, including the use of Ezra Pound's Mauberley as narrator, the inclusion of famous historical figures, the double framing device, the writing-on-the-wall motif, and what Eugene Benson calls the "fictionalization of history"

(D71). George Woodcock comments on the "sophistication of a literature that has come to the point where forms and artifices, parodies and
pastiches, are the serious concerns of serious writers" (D73). He also
sees this novel as a statement on the real character of history, the
meaning of evil, the sources of violence, and the nature and effect of
war. Dennis Duffy (C91) and Linda Hutcheon (C92) discuss the novel
as a postmodern fiction that explores the joint creative acts of writing
and reading. "The reader," Hutcheon writes, "becomes the actualizing
link between history and fiction." *Famous Last Words* was not published in Britain until 1987, after the death of the Duchess of Windsor
who is a prominent character in it. Negative British reviews, many of
them focusing on Findley's portrayal of the Duke and Duchess, appear
to have helped make the novel an overnight best-seller.

Findley's next two novels — *Not Wanted on the Voyage* (1984) and
The Telling of Lies (1986) — are experimental in form while continuing
to deal with the author's major themes and to articulate his vision. *Not
Wanted on the Voyage* is a blending of fact and fiction like Findley's
earlier novels, but, as George Woodcock writes, it is less a revision of
history than "the remythologization of a myth" (C100). John Moss,
calling the novel "a thing of wonder," writes that Findley discards the
conventions of genre and defies the rules of history and chronology
(C141). George Woodcock sees the novel as expressing a Gnostic view
of the natural order and the nature of God (C100, C135) while Ken
Adachi finds that Findley's "deliberately planted" anachronisms force
the story out of the distant past into the reader's present (D101). Read
as a metaphor for our own time, Findley addresses contemporary
concerns: the environment, society's treatment of the handicapped, and
the threat of nuclear war. Constance Rooke (D110) and W.J. Keith (D115)
stress the novel's feminist message. Alberto Manguel finds that Mrs.
Noyes and Mottyl express Findley's vision by representing a universal
memory that prevents the annihilation of life (D120).

Findley continued to experiment in form with *The Telling of Lies*. It
is his first murder mystery as well as the first time he has written entirely
in the first person, as an old woman. Vanessa is almost universally
acclaimed as an effective narrator. *The Telling of Lies* is also Findley's
most overtly political novel, expressing his concerns with relations
between the United States and Canada, powerful governments, and
complacent citizens. As Joel Yanofsky writes, Findley's style has
changed but his message is the same — "the corrupt alliance . . . between

evil and complacency" (D124). Findley calls it his "most nationalistic novel" (C134). He rejects the mystery novel label and says the book is more of a "howdunit" than a "whodunit" (C130, C159). Critics have also commented on the novel's prison imagery and the symbolism of its iceberg.

As well as his six novels, Timothy Findley has written short stories, plays, filmscripts, and done a great deal of work for radio and television. Findley's plays have received mixed reviews and are not often performed. John S. Bolin examines the use of irony and presentational staging techniques in *Can You See Me Yet?* (1976), which was written while Findley was the first playwright-in-residence at the National Arts Centre. These techniques enhance the themes of prudence, sacrifice, distrust of power, and national identity (C148). Findley wrote the screenplay for a film version of *The Wars* (1981), directed by Robin Phillips. Although the film was not a commercial success, it is considered an important event in Canadian filmmaking. As a writer for television, Findley is perhaps best known for his work on CBC Television's *The Whiteoaks of Jalna* (1972) and *The National Dream* (1974). Mary Jane Miller calls *The Paper People* (1967) a "superbly original work" (C75). This highly controversial drama was CBC Television's first feature-length film. More recently, Findley wrote and narrated a CBC Radio series on the music of Stephen Sondheim (1987) and adapted *Famous Last Words* for a five-part radio series (1988).

A collection of short fiction, *Dinner Along the Amazon*, was published in 1984. The stories in this collection span Findley's thirty-year writing career and had all been previously published or broadcast except the title story. Rona Murray notes that in these stories we can trace the development of Findley's writing skills as well as become aware of the repetitions in his imagery and subject matter: "The same voice speaks throughout. The voice becomes surer of itself" (D95). Don Murray discusses optical images in these stories, calling Findley's characters "intense spectators, and the spectacle they behold is frequently unusual, if not bizarre" (C157).

Of the nine stories in *Stones* (1988), Findley's second collection of short fiction, only four had been previously published, all within the previous year and a half. Rupert Schieder calls the stories in this collection the "latest bulletins from the world of Timothy Findley," pointing out the thematic consistency that links the stories to each other and to Findley's work as a whole (D143). The stories are set in Toronto and peopled by what Gillian Mackay calls "dream walkers treading dangerously close to madness" (D140). The title story, "Stones," is admired as the best in the collection by nearly all its reviewers. Neil Bissoondath, reviewing the collection, writes that Findley is "a writer of prodigious talents who, through an uncalculated modesty, maintains the illusion that he is a simple spinner of tales" (D142).

Timothy Findley is not a prolific writer, but, as Eugene Benson writes, "he has written only masterpieces" (D71). Findley's comments in interviews on the writing process attest to the care and craftsmanship that go into each page as well as to the combination of hard work, emotional involvement, and joy from which his work is created. Benson places Findley in the "very front ranks of contemporary novelists" (D71).

ACKNOWLEDGEMENTS

Many people have helped us with the compilation of this bibliography. We were delighted with the prompt and helpful responses we received from librarians, archivists, and scholars all over the country. We would like to especially acknowledge the kind assistance of Jack David, Robert Lecker, and Ellen Quigley of ECW PRESS; Leone Earls, Gail Donald, Ken Puley, and Martin von Mirbach of the CBC; Laureen Cusack of the Colbert Agency; Anne Johnston of the CNIB National Library; Anne Goddard of the National Archives of Canada; the Readers for the Canadian Federation for the Humanities; and Catherine Ross, at the School of Library and Information Science, the University of Western Ontario. Our families, friends, and co-workers in the Reference Department of the D.B. Weldon Library have been patient with our obsession, encouraging when we became discouraged, and provided us with a great deal of help.

Timothy Findley and William Whitehead have given us invaluable assistance in verifying foreign book editions, providing difficult-to-find material, allowing us access to the material in the National Archives collection, and inviting us to "delve into" the twenty-some scrapbooks in Timothy Findley's possession. The afternoon we spent at their home, Stone Orchard, was personally delightful as well as bibliographically profitable. Their continuing interest and encouragement have made this project a memorable and rewarding experience.

I

Works by Timothy Findley

A Books (Novels, Short Stories, and Plays), Play Productions, Films, Audio-Visual Material, and Manuscripts

Novels

A1 *The Last of the Crazy People.* London: Macdonald, 1967. 282 pp.
_____ . New York: Meredith, 1967. 282 pp.
_____ . Toronto: General, 1967. 282 pp.
_____ . New York: Bantam, 1968. 218 pp.
_____ . Toronto: Bantam, 1968. 218 pp.
_____ . London: Corgi, 1969. 218 pp.
_____ . Toronto: Macmillan, 1977. 282 pp.
_____ . Markham, Ont.: Penguin, 1983. 282 pp.
_____ . New York: Laurel/Dell, 1985. 282 pp.

A2 *The Butterfly Plague.* London: André Deutsch, 1969. 376 pp.
_____ . New York: Viking, 1969. 376 pp.
_____ . Toronto: Macmillan, 1969. 376 pp.
_____ . New York: Bantam, 1970. 340 pp.
_____ . Toronto: Bantam, 1970. 340 pp.
_____ . London: Corgi, 1972. 340 pp.
_____ . Rev. ed. Preface Timothy Findley. Markham, Ont.: Penguin, 1986. i–iv, 374 pp.

A3 *The Wars.* Toronto: Clarke, Irwin, 1977. 226 pp.
Der Krieg und die Kröte: Roman. Trans. Annemarie Böll. Munchen: R. Piper, 1978. 270 pp.

The Wars. London: Macmillan, 1978. 226 pp.

_____ . Markham, Ont.: Penguin, 1978. 190 pp.

_____ . New York: Delacorte/Seymour Lawrence, 1978. 226 pp.

De Eeuwige Oorlog: Roman. Trans. J. Sluistra. Amsterdam: Meulenhoff, 1979. 224 pp.

Las Guerras. Trans. Carlos Gardini. Buenos Aires: Sudamericana, 1979. 210 pp.

Guerres: Roman. Trans. Eric Diacon. Paris: Fayard, 1979. 255 pp.

Krigen. Trans. Trygve Greiff. Oslo: J.W. Cappelens, 1979. 213 pp.

The Wars. Harmondsworth, Eng.: Penguin, 1979. 191 pp.

_____ . New York: Dell, 1979. 254 pp.

Guerres: Roman. Trans. Eric Diacon. LaSalle, P.Q.: HMH, 1980. 272 pp.

Der Krieg und die Kröte: Roman. Trans. Annemarie Böll. Frankfurt am Main: Fischer, 1980. 205 pp.

Krigen. Trans. Brita Dahlman. Stockholm: Norstedt, 1980. 238 pp.

Sota. Trans. Risto Lehmusoksa. Jyväskylä: Gummerus, 1980. 224 pp.

The Wars. Braille ed. Toronto: CNIB, 1980.

_____ . New York: Dell, 1983. 254 pp.

See A15 and B93.

A4 *Famous Last Words.* Toronto: Clarke, Irwin, 1981. 396 pp.

Skriften På Väggen. Stockholm: Norstedt, 1981. 391 pp.

Famous Last Words. Markham, Ont.: Penguin, 1982. 396 pp.

_____ . New York: Delacorte/Seymour Lawrence, 1982. 396 pp.

_____ . New York: Dell, 1983. 396 pp.

De Laatste Onvergankelijke Woorden: Roman. Trans. Piet Verbagen. Amsterdam: Meulenhoff, 1983. 410 pp.

De Sidste Ord. Trans. Ib Christiansen. Copenhagen: Forum, 1983. 287 pp.

Famous Last Words. Braille ed. Toronto: CNIB, 1986.

Le Grand Elysium Hotel. Trans. Bernard Géniès. Paris: Robert Laffont, 1986. 383 pp.

Famous Last Words. London: Macmillan, 1987. 396 pp.

Viimeiset Sanat. Trans. Hanno Vammelvuo and Alice Martin. Jyväskylä: Gummerus, 1987. 465 pp.

Famous Last Words. Large Print ed. Oxford: Clio, 1988. 556 pp.

See B101.

A5 *Not Wanted on the Voyage.* Markham, Ont.: Viking, 1984. 352 pp.
A Bordo con Noè. Trans. Ettore Capriolo. Milano: Garzanti, 1985.
363 pp.
Not Wanted on the Voyage. London: Macmillan, 1985. 352 pp.
_____ . Markham, Ont.: Penguin, 1985. 352 pp.
_____ . New York: Delacorte, 1985. 352 pp.
_____ . Braille ed. Toronto: CNIB, 1986.
_____ . London: Arrow, 1986. 352 pp.
Suuri Tulva. Trans. Hanno Vammelvuo and Alice Martin. Jyväskylä:
Gummerus, 1986. 396 pp.
Not Wanted on the Voyage. New York: Dell, 1987. 343 pp.

A6 *The Telling of Lies: A Mystery.* Markham, Ont.: Viking, 1986.
359 pp.
_____ . Markham, Ont.: Penguin, 1987. 359 pp.
_____ . London: Macmillan, 1988. 359 pp.
_____ . New York: Dell, 1988. 359 pp.
See B94.

Short Stories

A7 *Dinner Along the Amazon.* Introd. Timothy Findley. Penguin Short
Fiction. Harmondsworth, Eng.: Penguin, 1984. ix–xxii, 253 pp.
_____ . Introd. Timothy Findley. Penguin Short Fiction. Markham,
Ont.: Penguin, 1984. ix–xxii, 253 pp.
Includes "About Effie" (B1), "The Book of Pins" (B5), "Daybreak at
Pisa" (B12), "Dinner Along the Amazon," "Hello Cheeverland, Good-
bye" (B6), "Lemonade" (B11), "Losers, Finders, Strangers at the Door"
(B7), "Out of the Silence" (B13), "The People on the Shore" (see B92),
"Sometime — Later — Not Now" (B4), "War" (see B78), "What Mrs.
Felton Knew" (B3).

A8 *Stones.* Markham, Ont.: Penguin, 1988. 221 pp.
Includes "Almeyer's Mother" (B19), "Bragg and Minna" (B18),
"Dreams," "Foxes" (B17), "A Gift of Mercy," "The Name's the Same"
(B16), "Real Life Writes Real Bad," "The Sky," and "Stones."

3

Plays

A9 *Can You See Me Yet?*. Introd. Margaret Laurence. Talonplays. Ed. Peter Hay. Vancouver: Talonbooks, 1977. 9-13, 166 pp.

Play Productions

A10 *Can You See Me Yet?*. Dir. Marigold Charlesworth. National Arts Centre, Ottawa. 1-20 March 1976.

The cast is Edward Atienza, Laurence Aubrey, Helen Burns, Clare Coulter, Maggie Griffin, Amelia Hall, William Hutt, Frances Hyland, Judy Marshak, Larry Reynolds, and William Webster.

A11 *John A. — Himself!*. Dir. Peter Moss. Theatre London, London, Ont. 31 Jan.–17 Feb. 1979.

The cast is Mark Bolton, Michael Carvana, Eric Donkin, M.E. Evans, Abraham Guenther, William Hutt, Robert LaChance, Tom McCamus, Stephen Ouimette, Jennifer Phipps, Jacquie Presley, Jack Roberts, Ralph Small, Peggy Watson, and Richard Whelan.

Films

A12 *Don't Let the Angels Fall*. Prod. John Kemeny. Dir. George Kaczender. National Film Board, 1969. (16mm.; black-and-white; 98 min., 55 sec.)

A13 *The Newcomers 1832*. Prod. Gordon Hinch. Dir. John McGreevey. Nielsen-Ferns, 1978. (16mm.; colour; 59 min.)
See B9 ("Island").

A14 *The Newcomers 1911*. Prod. Gordon Hinch. Dir. Eric Till. Nielsen-Ferns, 1978. (16mm.; colour; 58 min.)
See B10 ("A Long Hard Walk").

A15 *The Wars*. Prod. Richard Nielsen. Dir. Robin Phillips. Nielsen-Ferns and National Film Board, 1981. (16mm.; colour; 120 min., 1 sec.)
See A3 and B93.

Audio-Visual Material

A16 *The Wars*. Narr. Frank Herbert. Talking Books. Toronto: CNIB, 1977. (5 cassettes, 2–track, 7 hr. 30 min.; and 2 cassettes, 4–track, 6 hr.)

A17 *Famous Last Words.* Narr. Frank Herbert. Talking Books. Toronto: CNIB, 1981. (12 cassettes, 2–track, 15 hr., 50 min.; and 3 cassettes, 4–track, 13 hr., 15 min.)

A18 *Dinner Along the Amazon.* Narr. Mike Kramer. Talking Books. Toronto: CNIB, 1984. (8 cassettes, 2–track, 12 hr.; and 2 cassettes, 4–track, 11 hr.)

A19 *Not Wanted on the Voyage.* Narr. Mike Kramer. Talking Books. Toronto: CNIB, 1984. (10 cassettes, 2–track, 15 hr.; and 3 cassettes, 4–track, 14 hr., 45 min.)

A20 *The Telling of Lies.* Narr. Aileen Seaton. Talking Books. Toronto: CNIB, 1986. (9 cassettes, 2–track, 13 hr., 30 min.; and 3 cassettes, 4–track, 12 hr., 50 min.)

Manuscripts

A21 Timothy Findley Papers (MG 31 D196)
The National Archives of Canada
Ottawa, Ontario

Note: The Timothy Findley Papers were acquired by the National Archives in January 1987, with additional materials received in March 1988. The collection is not yet fully processed and restrictions on parts of it are still being negotiated. With the exception of the Literary Manuscripts Series, the following list is based on the arrangement of the collection in May 1988. Volume numbers may change as processing continues. Information regarding use of the collection is available from Anne Goddard at the Archives. In general, a volume consists of one 20 cm. (8 in.) file box.

LITERARY MANUSCRIPTS SERIES

Note: This part of the collection is fully processed and will be open for research purposes. A Finding Aid (No. 1731) has been prepared and is available at the Archives. Volume numbers and entry format for this part of the collection are based on its final arrangement as reflected in the Finding Aid, prepared in October 1988. Titles refer to novels unless otherwise noted.

Vols. 1-4 *The Last of the Crazy People*: notes, manuscripts, typescripts, correspondence, galleys, notebooks; film script version manuscripts and typescripts, notes, correspondence, and clippings. "Nobody Waved Goodbye": manuscript, typescript, notebooks, related correspondence, and dialogue continuity for film script version.

Vols. 5-8 *The Butterfly Plague*: notes, notebooks, manuscripts, typescripts, correspondence, galleys, proofs, reviews; revised edition typescripts.

Vols. 9-15 "Desperadoes" (also called "Wild Buffalo Park," "Birds of Prey," "Birds of Prayer," "Genesis 126," and "Olivia, Michael, Clair"): manuscripts, outline, notes, notebooks, and typescripts; "Getting it Home": typescript; "Whimper," (also called "Through the River Singing"): manuscripts, notes, notebooks, and related correspondence; play version: manuscripts, typescripts, and outline.

Vols. 16-17 *The Wars*: notes, notebooks, manuscripts, typescripts, correspondence, resource material, galleys, touring copy, and annotations; radio script version typescript.

Vols. 18-19 Film *The Wars*: outline, typescript, notes, and production material.

Vols. 20-30 *Famous Last Words*: notes, manuscripts, typescripts, notebooks, correspondence, outline, publication material, resource material, and promotional tour material.

Vols. 31-34 *Not Wanted on the Voyage*: manuscripts, typescripts, notes, proofs, and edited excerpts for promotional tour.

Vols. 35-36 *The Telling of Lies*: outline, notes, typescripts, rejected pages, excerpt as published in *The Canadian Forum*, correspondence, page proofs, bound proofs, cover design, and resource material.

Vol. 37 Short story material submitted to Macmillan: typescript; *Dinner Along the Amazon* Introduction: notes and typescript; short story "Lemonade": manuscripts, notebook, and typescript; radio script "Watch Out for the World": typescript; television script "Nothing — Nothing" (also called "Lemonade" and "Empty Boxes"): manuscript, typescript, and film scripts. Short story "War": typescripts.

Vol. 38 Short story "About Effie": typescript; short story "Sometime — Later — Not Now": typescripts; "What Mrs. Felton Knew": typescripts and copy of *Cavalier* in which story was published; short story "The People on the Shore": manuscript and typescripts; short story "Hello Cheeverland, Goodbye": radio script, manuscripts, notebooks, notes, and typescript.

Vols. 39-40 Short story "Losers, Finders, Strangers at the Door": manuscript, typescripts, related correspondence, photocopy of story as published in *75: New Canadian Stories*, and typescripts of play "The Killing of Strangers"; short story "The Book of Pins": typescript; short story "Out of the Silence": typescript; short story "Dinner Along the Amazon": notes, manuscript, and typescript. Uncollected short stories (untitled and various titles): manuscripts, typescripts, resource material, and notebooks. Novella "Rescue": notes, manuscripts, and notebooks; television script "Too Cold for Hell": outlines.

Vol. 41 Plays (untitled and various titles): manuscripts, typescripts, notebooks, resource material, and related correspondence.

Vols. 42-45 Play *Can You See Me Yet?*: television versions entitled "Promise," "Memoir," "The Conditions of the Exile": outlines, notes, manuscripts, and typescripts; play versions "Guns" and "Missionaries": notebooks, manuscripts, related correspondence, radio version, and typescripts; play *Can You See Me Yet?*: notes, typescripts, theatre programme, notebooks, and manuscripts.

Vols. 46-47 Play *John A. — Himself!*: correspondence, notes, notebooks, typescripts, manuscripts, script as performed opening night, resource material, and review; play *Piaf*: typescripts, resource material, related correspondence, and notes.

Vol. 48 Film *Don't Let the Angels Fall*: typescripts, notes, outlines, and manuscripts.

Vol. 49 Film "Killing Ground": typescripts, resource material, and copy of novel on which it is based; film "Venom": outline and notes. Television dramas (untitled and various titles): outlines, notes, typescripts, and scripts.

Vol. 50 Television drama *The Paper People*: manuscripts and typescripts of short story version, notes, notebook, outlines, typescripts, manuscripts, scripts, production material, reviews, interviews, and resource material.

Vol. 51 Television dramas "A Certain Grave," "The Last Thing You Hear Is Silence," and "Arnold": manuscripts, typescripts, resource material, and notes.

Vols. 52-57 Television drama *The Whiteoaks of Jalna*: notes, notebooks, related correspondence, outlines, manuscripts, typescripts, scripts, inserts of new material, production material, reviews, publicity, and resource material including 17 Mazo de la Roche novels used in adaptation.

Vols. 58-63 Television drama *The National Dream*: notes, notebooks, historical notes, outlines, Pierre Berton's notes and comments, editing notes, editing scripts, typescripts, scripts, production material, and resource material.

Vols. 64-66 Television drama "Klondike": notes, outlines, typescript, editing scripts, and resource material including several books.

Vol. 67 Television drama "Seascope": notes and outline; television drama "Whisper" (also called "Bishops"): notes, manuscript, notebook, and typescript; television drama *Royal Suite*: outline and typescript; television drama "Sidestreet": typescripts and scripts; television drama *Catsplay*: typescript, notes, and resource material; television drama "Are You Now — Or Have You Ever Been": notes, outline, typescript, and resource material; television drama "Incidents in the Life of Bob Edwards": outline; television drama *Other People's Children*: typescripts and scripts.

Vol. 68 Television drama *The Newcomers*: notes, typescripts, inserts, resource material, manuscript, and notebook.

Vol. 69 Television documentary "The Golden Age": outline; television documentary "The Story Goes": notes and outline; television documentaries for *Show on Shows/Umbrella* series (on Raymond Souster, Michelangelo Antonioni and Ingmar Bergman, Ulysse Comtois, William Hutt, and Michael Langham): outlines, typescripts, scripts, and resource material; for *Extension* Series ("Poets Here, Now and Then" and "The Garden and the Cage"): script, related correspondence, resource material.

Vols. 70-71 Television documentary *Dieppe 1942*: scripts and resource material; television special *Belafonte Sings*: notes, outlines, correspondence, manuscripts, scripts, production material, and resource material.

Vols. 72-75 Radio material (untitled and various titles) including "To Please the Millions," "Composers in the World Today," "Canadian Playwrights," "Canadian Composers," and "Seven Canadian Novelists": notes, manuscripts, typescripts, resource material, and scripts.

Vols. 76-77 Poetry (untitled and various titles): notes, manuscripts, and typescripts; other writing (untitled and various titles) including *Globe and Mail* article on *Hamlet* tour and "Alice Drops Her Cigarette on the Floor": notes, manuscripts, and typescripts.

Vols. 78-80 (Oversize) *The Wars*: book jacket, resource material, and notes; *Famous Last Words*: notes, notebooks, galleys, book jacket design, and resource material; *The Telling of Lies*: resource material;

various television and radio dramas: reviews, publicity, resource material, and notes; poetry: manuscripts.

Note: Volume numbers beyond Vol. 80 are tentative. Missing volume numbers 81-83 are the result of renumbering during processing of the Literary Manuscripts Series.

CORRESPONDENCE SERIES

Note: This part of the collection is not yet fully processed. It is expected that there will be restrictions on its use by researchers.

Vols. 84-97 Alphabetically arranged correspondence up to 1983. Correspondents include writers, actors, critics, publishers, organizations, the CBC, family, friends, and individuals requesting money, interviews, and readings. Approximately three volumes contain material relating to the Writers' Union of Canada. Also included are some articles, programmes, clippings, calendars, invitations, business records, awards, and papers relating to Findley's residence.

FINANCIAL ACCOUNTS SERIES

Note: This part of the collection is not yet fully processed.

Vols. 98-109 Includes business and personal accounts, financial records, and related correspondence for Timothy Findley, William Whitehead, and Pebble Productions for 1963-83.

PERSONAL JOURNALS SERIES

Note: This part of the collection is not yet fully processed. It is expected that there will be restrictions on its use by researchers.

Vols. 110-14 Includes personal journals, appointment calendars, address books, and a few clippings for 1955-83.

MANUSCRIPTS BY OTHERS, CLIPPINGS, REVIEWS, AND MISCELLANEOUS SERIES

Note: This part of the collection is not yet fully processed.

Vols. 115-17 Manuscripts submitted to Timothy Findley to read or review. Includes work by James Anderson, George Bloomfield, Barry Callaghan, John Coulter, Grace Morris Craig, Patrick Cumming,

Graeme Gibson, Roy MacGregor, Matthew Mackey, Janis Rapoport, Heather Robertson, and Scott Symons.

Vols. 118-21 Copies of periodicals containing articles by or about Timothy Findley and reviews of his books, plays, and films; clippings from magazines and newspapers of same; some publishers' catalogues and brochures; and theatre programmes.

Vol. 122 Miscellaneous. Includes annotated scripts of *The Matchmaker* and *Hamlet*, theatre programmes, typescript of a play adaptation of *The Brothers Karamazov* by Alec Guinness, and a copy of *The Theatre* (1882) presented to Timothy Findley.

RECENT ACQUISITIONS SERIES

Note: This part of the collection was received in March 1988 and is not yet fully processed. It is expected that there will be restrictions on its use by researchers.

Vols. 123-33 Alphabetically arranged correspondence for 1984-86, with a small amount of material from earlier years. Includes some journals, appointment calendars, publishers' catalogues, copies of articles, clippings, speeches, theatre programmes, reviews, travel brochures, curriculum vitae, and book jackets.

Vols. 134-37 Accounts and financial statements for Pebble Productions, 1982-86.

PHOTOGRAPHS AND DRAWINGS SERIES

Note: This part of the collection will be housed in the Documentary Art and Photography Division of the National Archives.

Vol. 138 Photographs. Includes professional proofs, colour slides, snapshots, photographs used in promotional material, and negatives, done by Timothy Findley and others.

Vol. 139 Drawings. Includes a sketchbook, watercolours, portraits, and sketches done by Timothy Findley.

AUDIO TAPES SERIES

Note: This part of the collection consists of approximately 200 reel-to-reel audio tapes (3.75", 5", and 7.5") and is housed at the Moving Image and Sound Division of the National Archives. It is not yet processed.

CBC Material: Many of the tapes are of CBC Radio programmes broadcast between 1963 and 1973. Some have notes or announcer instructions in the boxes. The CBC tapes include the following programmes and series, listed in approximate chronological order: "The Show That Is" (48 tapes), "The National Ballet of Canada" (8 tapes), "Taping Stratford" (8 tapes), "Canadian Playwrights" (13 tapes), "Children of Dionysus" (1 tape), "Music and Theatre" (13 tapes), "Method of Madness" (1 tape), "Canadian Composers" (1 tape), "Letter on Damien" (1 tape), "Adrift: A Monologue Inside Space" (1 tape), "The Journey" (1 tape), "Conversation Piece" (33 tapes), "Missionaries" (1 tape), and "River Through Time" (1 tape).

Miscellaneous: Also in the collection are approximately 35 music tapes (classical, pop, show tunes, and folk music); 11 tapes of resource material for CBC programmes; 1 audition tape (Findley reading the story "War"); 1 tape of radio advertisements; 1 tape describing a family trip; and 1 tape of poetry sent to Findley by a fan, with a letter in the box.

A22 *Canadian Literature* Files
W.H. New, Editor
The University of British Columbia
Vancouver, British Columbia
The *Canadian Literature* Files contain the typescript of an article by
Timothy Findley for *Canadian Literature* and correspondence from him
to W.H. New.

A23 John F. Hulcoop
Department of English
The University of British Columbia
Vancouver, British Columbia
Professor Hulcoop's collection contains 12 letters and some cards from
Timothy Findley to John F. Hulcoop, including one in which he dis-
cusses the progress of *Not Wanted on the Voyage*.

A24 The Dennis Lee Papers
Thomas Fisher Rare Book Library
The University of Toronto
Toronto, Ontario
The Dennis Lee Papers contain six letters from Timothy Findley to
Dennis Lee, 1977-79.

A25 Fonds Gabrielle Roy Collection
National Library of Canada
Ottawa, Ontario
The Fonds Gabrielle Roy Collection contains three letters from
Timothy Findley to Gabrielle Roy, 1978-79.

A26 Chris Scott Papers
National Library of Canada
Ottawa, Ontario
The Chris Scott Papers contain two letters from Timothy Findley to
Chris Scott, 1981.

A27 The Margaret Laurence Papers
York University Archives
Downsview, Ontario
The Margaret Laurence Papers contain correspondence from Timo-
thy Findley to Margaret Laurence. Access to this collection is restricted.

A28   Amelia Hall Papers
      National Archives of Canada
      Ottawa, Ontario
The Amelia Hall Papers contain letters from Timothy Findley to Amelia Hall.

A29   Robert Weaver Papers
      National Archives of Canada
      Ottawa, Ontario
The Robert Weaver Papers contain letters from Timothy Findley to Robert Weaver, 1978-82.

A30   The Alice Munro Papers
      The University of Calgary Library
      Calgary, Alberta
The Alice Munro Papers contain one letter from Timothy Findley to Alice Munro (10 Jan. 1983).

A31   Hugh Hood Archive
      The University of Calgary Library
      Calgary, Alberta
The Hugh Hood Archive contains one letter from Timothy Findley to Hugh Hood (9 Oct. 1968).

A32   The *Quill & Quire* Collection
      National Library of Canada
      Ottawa, Ontario
The *Quill & Quire* Collection contains two photographs of Timothy Findley, one by Arnaud Maggs and the other by Paul Orenstein.

B Contributions to Periodicals and Books (Short Stories and Excerpts, Scripts, Articles, Reprinted Anthology Contributions: A Selection, Book Reviews, and Miscellaneous), Radio Material, and Television Material

Note: When an item is reprinted in one of Timothy Findley's books, this fact is noted in the entry by the use of one of the following abbreviations:

The Butterfly Plague	*BP*
Dinner Along the Amazon	*DAA*
Famous Last Words	*FLW*
Not Wanted on the Voyage	*NWV*
Stones	*Stones*
The Telling of Lies	*TL*
The Wars	*Wars*

Short Stories and Excerpts

B1 "About Effie." *The Tamarack Review*, No. 1 (Autumn 1956), pp. 48-60. *DAA.*

B2 "Chronicle of the Nightmare." *Esquire* [New York], April 1969, pp. 140, 158, 160, 162, 166, 172, 174. *BP* (expanded — "The Chronicle of the Nightmare").

B3 "ERA." *Cavalier* [Greenwich, Conn.], April 1970, pp. 30-32, 74-77. *DAA* ("What Mrs. Felton Knew").

B4 "Sometime — Later — Not Now." *The New Orleans Review* [Loyola Univ., New Orleans], 3, No. 1 (1972), 13-20. *DAA.*

B5 "The Book of Pins." In *74: New Canadian Stories.* Ed. David Helwig and Joan Harcourt. Ottawa: Oberon, 1974, pp. 111-24. *DAA.*

B6 "Hello Cheeverland, Goodbye." *The Tamarack Review*, No. 64 (Nov. 1974), pp. 14-50. *DAA* (revised).

B7 "Losers, Finders: Strangers at the Door." In *75: New Canadian Stories.* Ed. David Helwig and Joan Harcourt. Ottawa: Oberon, 1975, pp. 57-75. *DAA* (revised — "Losers, Finders, Strangers at the Door").

B8 "From *The Wars: A Novel.*" *Exile*, 4, Nos. 3-4 (1977), 10-26. *Wars* (expanded — One: Sec. Prologue, 1-10).

B9 "Island." In *The Newcomers: Inhabiting a New Land*. Ed. Charles E. Israel. Toronto: McClelland and Stewart, 1979, pp. 85-95. Rpt. trans. Yvan Steenhout ("Une Île") in *Les Arrivants: Habitants d'un Nouveau Monde*. Montréal: l'Homme, 1979, pp. 85-97.
See A13 (*The Newcomers 1832*).

B10 "A Long Hard Walk." In *The Newcomers: Inhabiting a New Land*. Ed. Charles E. Israel. Toronto: McClelland and Stewart, 1979, pp. 145-55. Rpt. trans. Yvan Steenhout ("Au Bout du Chemin") in *Les Arrivants: Habitants d'un Nouveau Monde*. Montréal: l'Homme, 1979, pp. 145-57.
See A14 (*The Newcomers 1911*).

B11 "Harper's Bazaar." *Exile*, 7, Nos. 1-2 (1980), 141-200. *DAA* (revised — "Lemonade").

B12 "Daybreak at Pisa: 1945: Excerpt from a Work-in-Progress." *The Tamarack Review*, Nos. 83-84 (Winter 1982), pp. 90-97. *DAA* ("Daybreak at Pisa").

B13 "Out of the Silence." *Ethos*, 1, No. 1 (Summer 1983), 26-28. *DAA*.

B14 "Draft Manuscript from *The Butterfly Plague*" [p. 269]. In *Writer's Craft*. Ed. Diane Brown. Toronto: Association of Large School Boards in Ontario, 1986, p. 523. *BP* (expanded — "The Chronicle of the Wish").

B15 "Focal Point: Fiction (From a Work-in-Progress)." *The Canadian Forum*, Feb. 1986, pp. 26-30. *TL* (expanded — Chs. xvi–xxviii).

B16 "The Name's the Same." *Grain*, 15, No. 1 (Feb. 1987), 16-24. *Stones*.

B17 "Foxes." *Rotunda*, 20, No. 1 (Summer 1987), 26-32. *Stones*.

B18 "Bragg and Minna." *The Malahat Review* [Univ. of Victoria], No. 80 (Fall 1987), pp. 5-22. *Stones*.

B19 "Almeyer's Mother." *Saturday Night*, June 1988, pp. 51-55, 70. *Stones*.

Scripts

B20   *Strangers at the Door. Quarry* [30th Anniversary Issue], 31, No. 3 (Summer 1982), 75-85.

B21   *The Paper People. Canadian Drama/L'Art dramatique canadien* [Univ. of Waterloo], 9 (1983), 63-164.

B22   *The Journey: A Montage for Radio. Canadian Drama/L'Art dramatique canadien* [Univ. of Waterloo], 10 (Spring 1984), 115-41.

B23   "From *John A. — Himself*" (excerpts). *Exile*, 11, No. 3 (1986), 24-37.

Articles

B24   "Never Look Down." *The Globe and Mail* [Toronto], 10 Dec. 1975, p. 41.

B25   "The Golden Age of Canadian Writing Is Here, Says a Writer. Respect It." *The Globe and Mail* [Toronto], 8 July 1978, p. 6.

B26   "Better Dead Than Read? An Opposing View." *Books in Canada*, Dec. 1978, pp. 3-5.

B27   "Christmas Remembered." *Chatelaine*, Dec. 1979, pp. 43, 80.

B28   "Critical Reaction No Factor in Award." Letter. *The Globe and Mail* [Toronto], 1 May 1980, p. 7.

B29   "A Determination to Be Heard." *The Graduate* [Univ. of Toronto], May–June 1980, pp. 18-19.

B30   "Alice Drops Her Cigarette on the Floor (William Whitehead Looking over Timothy Findley's Shoulder)." *Canadian Literature*, No. 91 (Winter 1981), pp. 10-21.

B31   "Mount Pleasant Cemetery." *Toronto Life*, April 1982, pp. 60-61, 83.

B32   "Prize–Winning Author Did Manual Labor: My First Job." As Told to Gord Gates. *The Toronto Star*, 27 July 1982, p. A2.

B33 "How Did Pinocchio Get into This?". *The Globe and Mail* [Toronto], 7 Aug. 1982, p. 6.

B34 "Some Films Are Books, and Some Books Are Films." *The Globe and Mail* [Toronto], 20 Nov. 1982, p. L1.

B35 _____ , and David Gardner. "On *The Paper People.*" *Canadian Drama/L'Art dramatique canadien* [Univ. of Waterloo], 9 (Spring 1983), 60-61.

B36 "Censorship by Any Other Name." *Indirections*, 8, No. 4 (Dec. 1983), 14-20.

B37 "The Countries of Invention." *Canadian Literature*, No. 100 (Spring 1984), pp. 104-08.

B38 "The King and Mrs. Simpson." *Toronto Life*, May 1984, pp. 32-33.

B39 "The Tea Party, or How I Was Nailed by Marian Engel, General Booth and Minn Williams Burge." *Room of One's Own* [Special Issue on Marian Engel], 9, No. 2 (June 1984), 35-40.

B40 "Marian Engel and The Tattooed Woman." In *The Tattooed Woman*. By Marian Engel. Penguin Short Fiction. Markham, Ont.: Penguin, 1985, pp. vii–ix.

B41 "Word Processing and the Writer." *Cross-Canada Writers' Quarterly*, 7, Nos. 3-4 (1985), 3-6.

B42 "In Memoriam: A Trial and a Joy." *Books in Canada*, April 1985, pp. 18-19.

B43 "Alarms and Excursions: Some Adventures in the Book Trade." *The Globe and Mail* [Toronto], 13 April 1985, "Books," p. 7.

B44 "My Mother, My Friend." *Chatelaine*, May 1985, pp. 46-47, 91.

B45 "Comparing Notes: Timothy Findley Shares Moments from the Sketchbooks of Isabel McLaughlin." *Canadian Art*, 7, No. 2 (Summer 1985), 54-57.

B46 "Mature Civil Wars." Letter. *The Globe and Mail* [Toronto], 27 July 1985, p. 7.
    See C122.

B47 "Riding Off in All Directions: A Few Wild Words in Search of Stephen Leacock." In *Stephen Leacock: A Reappraisal*. Ed. David Staines. Reappraisals: Canadian Writers, 12. Ottawa: Univ. of Ottawa Press, 1986, 5-9.

B48 "The Toughest Part of the Writing Process." In *Writer's Craft*. Ed. Diane Brown. Toronto: Association of Large School Boards in Ontario, 1986, pp. 518-22.

B49 "A Writer's Craft." *Grain* [Special Prose Issue], 14, No. 1 (Feb. 1986), 6-10.

B50 "Growing Up Together." *The Canadian Author & Bookman*, 61, No. 3 (Spring 1986), 6.

B51 "Legends." *Landfall: A New Zealand Quarterly* [Christchurch], 40 (Sept. 1986), 327-32.

B52 [Obituary on Margaret Laurence.] In *The New Morningside Papers*. Ed. Peter Gzowski. Toronto: McClelland and Stewart, 1987, pp. 218-20.
    See B95.

B53 "A Life of Eloquence and Radicalism." *Maclean's*, 19 Jan. 1987, pp. 52-53.
    Obituary on Margaret Laurence.

B54 "My Final Hour: An Address to the Philosophy Society, Trent University, Monday, 26 January 1987." *Journal of Canadian Studies/ Revue d'études canadiennes* [Trent Univ.], 22, No. 1 (Spring 1987), 5-16.

B55 "Writing: The Pain and Pleasure." *The Toronto Star*, 21 March 1987, "Books in Store for Spring," pp. M1, M5.

B56 "Margaret Laurence: A Remembrance." *Canadian Woman Studies/Les cahiers de la femme* [Centennial College], 8, No. 3 (Fall 1987), 14-15.

B57 Afterword. In *The Diviners*. By Margaret Laurence. New Canadian Library. Toronto: McClelland and Stewart, 1988, pp. 491-94.

B58 "Lana Speaks! C-54, Where Are You?". *This Magazine*, Feb. 1988, pp. 36-38.

Reprinted Anthology Contributions: A Selection

B59 "The Countries of Invention" (article). In *Canadian Writers in 1984*. Ed. W.H. New. Prefaces Edward R. Schreyer, Mavor Moore, and K. George Pedersen. Vancouver: Univ. of British Columbia Press, 1984, pp. 104-08.

B60 "Dinner Along the Amazon." In *The Oxford Book of Canadian Short Stories in English*. Ed. Margaret Atwood and Robert Weaver. Toronto: Oxford Univ. Press, 1986, pp. 179-90.

B61 "Jepeth Gets Marinated" (excerpt from *NWV* "Book 1") and "Supper in the Trenches" (excerpt from *Wars* "Two: 4"). In *The CanLit Foodbook: From Pen to Palate — A Collection of Tasty Literary Fare*. Ed. and illus. Margaret Atwood. Don Mills, Ont.: Totem, 1987, pp. 99-100, 169-70.

B62 "Bragg and Minna." In *88: Best Canadian Stories*. Ed. David Helwig and Maggie Helwig. [Ottawa]: Oberon, 1988, pp. 15-37.

Book Reviews

B63 "The Sweet Second Summer of Kitty Malone." Rev. of *The Sweet Second Summer of Kitty Malone*, by Matt Cohen. *The Globe and Mail* [Toronto], 3 March 1979, p. 44.

B64 "Beardless Mowat Goes to War." Rev. of *A Whale for the Killing*, by Farley Mowat. *Saturday Night*, Nov. 1979, pp. 40-42.

B65 "The Emergence of Toronto as a Place Beyond Its Concrete Self." Rev. of *The Black Queen Stories*, by Barry Callaghan. *The Globe and Mail* [Toronto], 24 April 1982, "Entertainment," p. 15.

B66 "Cast Off on Another Elba." Rev. of *The Duke of Windsor's War*, by Michael Bloch. *The Globe and Mail* [Toronto], 14 May 1983, "Entertainment," p. 18.

B67 Rev. of *The Whole Night, Coming Home*, by Roo Borson. *Journal of Canadian Poetry*, 1 (1986), 10-12.

B68 "Through the Looking Glass." Rev. of *Storm Glass*, by Jane Urquhart. *Books in Canada*, June–July 1987, p. 14.

B69 "Queen of the Apes." Rev. of *Virunga: The Passion of Dian Fossey*, by Farley Mowat. *Books in Canada*, Nov. 1987, pp. 16-17.

Miscellaneous

B70 "Beastly History" (descriptive prose). In *Imaginings: A Synthesis of Fact and Fable*. Ed. Robert Burns. Illus. Heather Cooper. Poetry Janis Rapoport. Toronto: Ethos Cultural Development Foundation, 1982, n. pag.

B71 "Metaphysic Monster" (descriptive prose). In *Imaginings: A Synthesis of Fact and Fable*. Ed. Robert Burns. Illus. Heather Cooper. Poetry Janis Rapoport. Toronto: Ethos Cultural Development Foundation, 1982, n. pag.

B72 "Perpetual Lyric" (descriptive prose). In *Imaginings: A Synthesis of Fact and Fable*. Ed. Robert Burns. Illus. Heather Cooper. Poetry Janis Rapoport. Toronto: Ethos Cultural Development Foundation, 1982, n. pag.

B73 "Philosophic Front" (descriptive prose). In *Imaginings: A Synthesis of Fact and Fable*. Ed. Robert Burns. Illus. Heather Cooper. Poetry Janis Rapoport. Toronto: Ethos Cultural Development Foundation, 1982, n. pag.

B74 "Scandals" (programme notes). In *Stratford Festival 1987 Performance Programme*. Stratford, Ont.: Stratford Festival, 1987, n. pag.

B75 "Timothy Findley's Summer Peaches" (recipe). In *The CanLit Foodbook: From Pen to Palate — A Collection of Tasty Literary Fare*. Ed. and illus. Margaret Atwood. Don Mills, Ont.: Totem, 1987, p. 120.

B76 "Murder in Our Time" (programme notes). In *Stratford Festival 1988 Performance Programme*. Stratford, Ont.: Stratford Festival, 1988, n. pag.

B77 "Stratters, Ont." (essay). In *Festive Stratford: 1988 Visitors' Guide*. Stratford, Ont.: Stratford Festival and Stratford and Area Visitors' and Convention Bureau, 1988, p. 4.

Radio Material

Note: Although Timothy Findley has written extensively for radio, a comprehensive record of his work is difficult to establish and verify. The CBC Program Archives (90 Sumach Street, Toronto) maintains a card catalogue of their holdings, but entries are incomplete for some years. Sean Francis Berrigan's *"Anthology:* Catalogue and Index 1954-1974, With a Critical Introduction" (available at CBC Program Archives) contains information on Findley's contributions to the *Anthology* series. The CBC Reference Library (365 Church Street, Toronto) has material that helps identify and date some of Findley's radio work. The entries in this section, and in section C (Interviews), are based on these sources. See the Timothy Findley Papers, National Archives, Literary Manuscripts Series and Audio Tapes Series (A21) for additional radio material.

B78 "War." Narr. Mavor Moore. *Anthology.* Prod. Robert McCormack. Ed. and introd. Robert Weaver. CBC Radio, 4 March 1958.
See *DAA.*

B79 "To Please the Millions." Narr. Tony van Bridge. CBC *Sunday Night.* Prod. James Kent. CBC Radio, 12 April 1964.
On the Canadian Players, a touring theatre company.

B80 "The Children of Dionysus." Narr. Leo Ciceri. Interviews with Louis Applebaum, Douglas Campbell, Bill Carter, Peter Cheyne, Jean Gascon, John Hirsch, Jack Hutt, William Hutt, Frances Hyland, Brian Jackson, Jane Needles, William Needles, Fred Nihda, Douglas Rain, Kate Reid, Mary Savidge, Martha Schlamme, Joseph Shaw, Grant Strate, Betty van Bridge, and Tony van Bridge. CBC Sunday Night. Prod. Bernard Murphy. CBC Radio, 25 July 1965. (55 min.)
Also called "Backstage at Stratford."

B81 "Seven Canadian Novelists." Interview with Austin Clarke. *The Best Ideas You'll Hear Tonight.* CBC-FM Radio, 28 Jan. 1966.

B82 "Seven Canadian Novelists." Interview with Hugh MacLennan. *The Best Ideas You'll Hear Tonight.* CBC-FM Radio, 4 Feb. 1966.

B83 "Seven Canadian Novelists." Interview with Charles Israel. *The Best Ideas You'll Hear Tonight.* CBC-FM Radio, 11 Feb. 1966.

B84 "Seven Canadian Novelists." Interview with Hugh Hood. *The*

Best Ideas You'll Hear Tonight. CBC-FM Radio, 18 Feb. 1966.

B85 "Seven Canadian Novelists." Interview with Leonard Cohen. *The Best Ideas You'll Hear Tonight.* CBC-FM Radio, 4 March 1966.

B86 "Walls — A Monologue Inside Space." Narr. Timothy Findley. *The Best of Ideas.* Prod. Janet Somerville. Exec. prod. Phyllis Webb. Host Ken Haslam. CBC-FM Radio, 24 June 1968.
A radio play on claustrophobia in which Findley plays the only character. Part 1 of series entitled *Inner Spaces.*

B87 "The Spatial Alice." Narr. Timothy Findley. *The Best of Ideas.* Host Ken Haslam. CBC-FM Radio, 5 Aug. 1968.
Readings from the work of Lewis Carroll.

B88 [On filming Margaret Laurence's *A Jest of God.*] Interview with Joan Fox. *Matinee.* Prod. Bill Castleman. Hosts Deb Holly, Pat Patterson, Ed Reid. CBC Radio, 6 Nov. 1968. (11 min.) Rebroadcast 7 Nov. 1968. (8 min.)

B89 "Missionaries." Narr. Mia Anderson, Ann Anglin, Robert Christie, Timothy Findley, Alice Hill, Danny McIlravey, Barry Morse, Karen Pearson, Barby Pierce, and Ruth Springfield. CBC *Tuesday Night.* Prod. James Anderson. CBC Radio, 22 Feb. 1972. (1 hr., 40 min.) Rebroadcast *Encore.* CBC-FM Radio, 2 March 1972. (1 hr., 40 min.)
Early version of *Can You See Me Yet?.*

B90 "River Through Time." Narr. Jackie Burroughs, Colin Fox, and Henry Ramer. *Ideas.* Prod. James Anderson. CBC-FM Radio, 20 April 1973. (57 min.) Rebroadcast 27 Aug. 1973. (57 min.)
A radio poem; the 9th and final programme in a series on rivers.

B91 "A Certain Limit." Narr. Jackie Burroughs, Jack Creley, and Timothy Findley. *Ideas.* Prod. James Anderson. CBC-FM Radio, 19 Nov. 1973.
A radio play describing a futuristic society.

B92 "The People on the Shore." Narr. Timothy Findley. *Anthology.* Ed. Robert Weaver. Announcer Harry Mannis. CBC Radio, 23 Feb. 1974. (32 min.)
See *DAA.*

B93 *The Wars* (excerpts). Narr. Timothy Findley. Adapted Alice Frick. *Booktime.* Prod. Eithne Black. cbc Radio, 29 Sept.–24 Oct. 1980. (20 parts; 15 min. each.)
See *Wars* and A15.

B94 *The Telling of Lies* (excerpts). Narr. Timothy Findley. *Mornings-ide.* Host Peter Gzowski. cbc Radio, 30 Oct. 1986.
See *TL.*

B95 [Obituary on Margaret Laurence.] Narr. Timothy Findley. *Morn-ingside.* Host Peter Gzowski. cbc Radio, 6 Jan. 1987.
See B52.

B96 "A Sense of Place." Narr. Timothy Findley. *State of the Arts.* Prod. Eithne Black. Host Shelagh Rogers. cbc-fm Radio, 5 July 1987.
Findley talks about his home and the community of Cannington, Ontario.

B97 "Personal Relationships: Part i, Timothy Findley's Stephen Sond-heim." Narr. Timothy Findley. *Arts National Friday Night.* Prod. Philip Coulter. Exec. prod. Rick Phillips. Host Terry Campbell. cbc-fm Radio, 13 Nov. 1987. (50 min.)

B98 "Memory: Part ii, Timothy Findley's Stephen Sondheim." Narr. Timothy Findley. *Arts National Friday Night.* Prod. Philip Coulter. Exec. prod. Rick Phillips. Host Terry Campbell. cbc-fm Radio, 20 Nov. 1987. (50 min.)

B99 "Harmony: Part iii, Timothy Findley's Stephen Sondheim." Narr. Timothy Findley. *Arts National Friday Night.* Prod. Philip Coulter. Exec. prod. Rick Phillips. Host Terry Campbell. cbc-fm Radio, 27 Nov. 1987. (50 min.)

B100 "Historical Sweep of a Society in Crisis: Part iv, Timothy Find-ley's Stephen Sondheim." Narr. Timothy Findley. *Arts National Friday Night.* Prod. Philip Coulter. Exec. prod. Rick Phillips. Host Terry Campbell. cbc-fm Radio, 4 Dec. 1987. (50 min.)

B101 "Famous Last Words." Adapted Timothy Findley. Narr. Jackie Burroughs, Steven Bush, Greg Ellwand, Donna Goodhand, Garrick

Hagon, Gary Reineke. *Sunday Matinee*. Prod. and dir. Damiano Pietro-paolo. CBC Radio, 10 Jan.–7 Feb., 1988. Rebroadcast on *Stereo Theatre*. CBC-FM Radio, 13 March–10 April 1988. (5 episodes; 50 min. each.) See *FLW*.

Television Material

Note: Although Timothy Findley has written extensively for television, a comprehensive record of his work is difficult to establish and verify. The CBC Program Archives (90 Sumach Street, Toronto) maintains a card catalogue of their holdings, but entries are incomplete for some years. The CBC Reference Library (365 Church Street, Toronto) and the Business Affairs Department (1255 Bay Street, Toronto) have material that helps identify and date some of Findley's work. The entries in this section, and in Section C (Interviews), are based on these sources. See the Timothy Findley Papers, National Archives, Literary Manuscripts Series (A21) for additional television material.

The National Dream, an eight-part series based on Pierre Berton's book and broadcast in March and April 1974, for which Findley and William Whitehead wrote the scripts, requires special comment. It is not included as an entry in this section because it was not possible to locate broadcast tapes for verification, but it is one of Findley's best-known works for television and is referred to in other sections of this bibliography. See Vols. 58-63 in the Timothy Findley Papers, National Archives, Literary Manuscript Series (A21).

B102 *A Portrait of Kate Reid*. Narr. Timothy Findley. *Show on Shows*. Prod. John L. Kennedy. Dir. Timothy Findley. CBC TV, 18 April 1965.

B103 *A Portrait of Michael Langham*. Narr. Timothy Findley. *The Umbrella*. Prod. John L. Kennedy. Host William Ronald. CBC TV, 5 June 1966.

B104 *A Portrait of William Hutt*. Narr. Timothy Findley. *The Umbrella*. Prod. John L. Kennedy. Host William Ronald. CBC TV, 26 June 1966.

B105 *Modern Canadian Poetry*. Narr. Timothy Findley. *Extension*. Prod. John L. Kennedy. Host Phyllis Webb. CBC TV, 4 June 1967.
Findley reads a selection of Raymond Souster's poetry.

B106 *The Paper People*. Dir. John Gardner. Cast: Marigold Charlesworth, Kate Reid, Brett Somers, Marc Strange, Robin Ward, Lucy Warner, Stevie Wise. CBC TV, 13 Dec. 1967. (90 min.)
cbc's first feature-length colour film.

B107 *The Whiteoaks of Jalna*. Prod. and dir. John Trent. Exec. Prod. Fletcher Markle. Cast: Antoinette Bower, Amelia Hall, Paul Harding, Don Scardino. Based on the novels of Mazo de la Roche. CBC TV, 23 Jan.–9 April 1972. (12 episodes; 60 min. each.)

B108 _____ , adapted. *Catsplay*. *Front Row Centre*. Prod. Beverley Roberts. Exec. Prod. Robert Allen. Cast: Helen Burns, Les Carlson, Moya Fenwick, Susan Fletcher, Angela Fusco, Rafe McPherson, Doris Petrie, Nancy Stewart. CBC TV, 1 March 1978. (90 min.)
Adapted from Istvan Orkeny's novel, *Catsplay*.

B109 *Other People's Children*. Cast: Les Carlson, Brett Davidson, Karen Finbow, Lynn Gorman, Pat Hamilton, Laurie Heifetz, Chris Makepeace, Doris Petrie. CBC TV, 28 March 1980.

2

Works on Timothy Findley

C Articles and Sections of Books, Theses and Dissertations, Interviews, Poems Dedicated to Timothy Findley, and Awards and Honours

Annotations by Carol Roberts

Articles and Sections of Books

C1 Whittaker, Herbert. "Flamboyant Personality an Aid to Russian Actor." *The Globe and Mail* [Toronto], 7 Dec. 1955, p. 7.

Findley was asked to give "an impression of Russian theatre today," based on his experience playing Osric in Paul Scofield's Moscow production of *Hamlet*. This article consists of his observations with a brief introduction and conclusion by Whittaker. Findley comments on the excellent production facilities, the experience of seeing a Russian play, and the "flamboyant" Russian personality. The only "tragedy" of Russian theatre is that "propaganda is the one tongue."

C2 Graham, June. "The Children of Dionysus." cBc Times, 24-30 July 1965, pp. 10-11.

Graham describes Findley's acting career, Ruth Gordon's influence, and his work for the cBc, where he is "particularly effective as an interviewer." His recently purchased farm near Cannington, Ontario is an "ideal setting . . . for his writing."

C3 Szende, Andrew. "Far from the Footlights Glory." *The Toronto Star*, 29 July 1967, p. 26.

Written just after publication of *The Last of the Crazy People*, this article profiles Findley's acting and writing careers. It incorrectly reports that Findley graduated from the University of Toronto. Findley left acting because of hardships he experienced during a year in Hollywood and because ". . . he doesn't think he was cut out to be an actor." He is optimistic about the future of Canadian writers and wants to write "The Great Canadian Novel."

C4   Hicklin, Ralph. "Paper People: A Step Up." *The Globe and Mail* [Toronto], 7 Oct. 1967, p. 19.

Hicklin calls *The Paper People*, the first film produced entirely by the CBC, "a movie that promises to be something of a landmark in the Canadian film industry." Findley's screenplay "will attract attention both for its novelty and for the extraordinary demands it makes on the film medium." In his original script the artist was a photographer, but after Findley saw the film *Blow Up* he changed this to avoid the obvious comparisons to Michelangelo Antonioni's film.

C5   "Scripting Paper People." *Montrealer*, March 1968, pp. 6-7.

This article traces Findley's involvement in writing the script for *The Paper People*. Unlike "traditional" writers, Findley realizes that words are secondary in the film medium. His use of symbolism is abstract and he describes things in a series of disconnected images. Findley was influenced by the films of Ingmar Bergman and Michelangelo Antonioni.

C6   Adilman, Sid. "No Entry for Nat'l Film Board at Can. Pic Awards, No Features at All." *Variety* [New York], 1 Oct. 1969, pp. 6, 66.

Findley's *Don't Let the Angels Fall*, premiered at the Cannes Film Festival, was withdrawn from competition in the Canadian Film Awards because of fear that not winning an award would hurt its chances commercially.

C7   Adilman, Sid. "Timothy Findley to Write CBC's Whiteoaks Series." *The Telegram* [Toronto], 17 Nov. 1970, p. 56.

In this article describing the upcoming CBC Television series *The Whiteoaks of Jalna*, Adilman names Findley as the writer contracted to write the pilot episode.

C8   S[tory]., N[ora]. "Findley, Timothy (1930)" and "Fiction in English 4." *Supplement to The Oxford Companion to Canadian History and*

Literature. Ed. William Toye. Toronto: Oxford Univ. Press, 1973.
The entry on Findley includes biographical information and briefly discusses the themes of his first two novels. Story notes that Findley's "mastery of theatre techniques lends great affectiveness" to his work. *The Butterfly Plague* is mentioned in the "Fiction in English 4" entry as a novel about man and society which "draws a parallel between the Nazi persecution of the Jews . . . and the ruthless manner in which Hollywood stars were made and unmade."

C9 "Playwright Hired at Arts Centre." *The London Free Press*, 5 Nov. 1974, p. 51.
Findley has been hired as playwright-in-residence at the National Arts Centre, with prospects of having his first play produced. He will follow "the full creative cycle" for a production of *Riel* by John Coulter while preparing his own script.

C10 Canada. National Arts Centre. *Annual Report: 1974-75*. Ottawa: Supply and Services, 1975, p. 24.
The National Arts Centre reports on its first playwright-in-residence programme. The report calls Findley an experienced actor and writer who "had the makings of a script but needed the chance to watch . . . the day-to-day business of making a play ready for the stage." "Living on a subsistence fee," Findley watched the production of John Coulter's *Riel* and finished his own play, *Can You See Me Yet?*, which will be produced next season. The National Arts Centre hopes to repeat its playwright-in-residence experiment.

C11 "Arts Centre to Produce Findley Play." *The Globe and Mail* [Toronto], 7 May 1975, p. 17.
The National Arts Centre will produce *Can You See Me Yet?*, written while Findley was playwright-in-residence. Findley came to the Centre "with a burning ambition to write for the stage, but no experience in how a play is put together."

C12 "Project Pays Off for Arts Centre." *The London Free Press*, 7 May 1975, p. 63.
Findley's first play, *Can You See Me Yet?*, is being produced at the National Arts Centre. Findley was hired for three months as playwright-in-residence to learn how a play is put together. During that time he wrote his script which is based on "a part of his own family experience."

C13 Canada. National Arts Centre. *Annual Report: 1975-76*. Ottawa: Supply and Services, 1976, p. 15.

The National Arts Centre reports that its 1975-76 season was distinguished by the world premiere of *Can You See Me Yet?*, which was written while Findley was its first playwright-in-residence. The "evocative" production featured "an unusually strong cast."

C14 Laurence, Margaret. "Margaret Laurence Talks About *Can You See Me Yet?*". *Stage*, March 1976, pp. 1-2, 4. Rpt. as Introduction in *Can You See Me Yet?*. Talonplays. Ed. Peter Hay. Vancouver: Talonbooks, 1977, pp. 9-13.

Can You See Me Yet? is "an astonishing work, richly textured, sombre, and yet possessing a relieving wit." Laurence describes the characters' double roles and praises Findley's skill in portraying character, particularly Cassandra's. The play poses difficult questions, but Findley does not attempt easy answers. Laurence identifies the play's themes and praises its complexity and dramatic force. "This is a play which will . . . continue to be performed in our theatres for a very long time to come."

C15 Laurence, Margaret. "Can You See Me Yet?". Letter. *The Globe and Mail* [Toronto], 10 March 1976, p. 7.

Laurence strongly disagrees with a review of *Can You See Me Yet?* published in *The Globe and Mail* (D146). She found the play "fascinating, powerful and of compelling interest."

C16 "Findley, Timothy 1930– ." *Contemporary Authors: A Bio-Bibliographical Guide to Current Authors and Their Works*. First Revision. Ed. Christine Nasso. Vols. xxv–xxviii. Detroit: Gale, 1977.

Includes biographical and bibliographical information and short quotations from reviews of *The Last of the Crazy People*.

C17 "Timothy Findley." *Canada Writes!* Ed. K.A. Hamilton. Toronto: Writers' Union of Canada, 1977.

Bibliographic information and a brief biography written by Findley. He comments on how he became a writer and on his interest in the novel and play genres.

C18 Callaghan, Barry. "Celebrating *The Wars* and Timothy Findley." *Toronto Life*, Dec. 1977, pp. 16-17.

Callaghan writes about a party celebrating publication of *The Wars*. Unlike most parties of this type, it was "open, full of laughter, affection and singing." He describes Findley's father and relates his conversation with other guests. Editor John Pearce and Margaret Laurence are present. Findley comments that every generation has a war; "the thing is not to take refuge in tragedy — but to clarify who you are . . . ."

C19 McFadden, David. "The Dead Stand Up in Their Graves . . . ." *Quill & Quire*, Dec. 1977, p. 17.

McFadden talks to Findley shortly before publication of *The Wars* about the novel and Findley's new role as chairman of the Writers' Union of Canada. Findley's ability to "capture that rare flavour" of the World War I era is "a remarkable achievement." Findley maintains that the novel is "pure fiction," not a *roman à clef*. Unlike his earlier books, this one is "what I wanted to say." It is more deliberately crafted, he adds, "not to make a lot of money, but to get read what I wanted to get read." McFadden comments on the violence in *The Wars* and Findley responds that ". . . there's a lot of violence in me." He lists Margaret Laurence, Carson McCullers, and Thorton Wilder as his favourite writers, and calls Wilder "a marvellous influence." He sees his work for the Writers' Union as a way of paying back in part what he owes to other writers.

C20 MacGregor, Roy. "Wound Stripes: Timothy Findley Poured All His Battles with Death and Life into Writing *The Wars*." *The Canadian*, 17 Dec. 1977, pp. 10-11.

Written shortly after publication of *The Wars*, this article describes Findley's difficulties getting his first two novels published, his lack of recognition in Canada, and his despair at being turned down by publishers. Findley is critical of Canadian critics who "dump on" Canadian writers. MacGregor describes the writing of *The Wars*, including Findley's experiences in a root cellar and a muddy field at his farm. Findley says for him violence is "an energy force," and that he is most angered by "the incredible intolerance surrounding us." MacGregor also describes Findley's childhood and the impression sickness and death made on him.

C21 "Toronto Book Award." *Quill & Quire*, 16 March 1978, p. 1.

An announcement of the 1978 City of Toronto Book Award winners. *The Wars* is one of two winning books.

C22 Adachi, Ken. "War Novel Wins Top Canadian Fiction Award." *The Toronto Star*, 1 May 1978, p. D1.

The Canada Council announces that *The Wars* has won the Governor General's Literary Award for best English-language work of fiction for 1977. The novel, which has received "rave reviews," has had modest sales but is destined for a wide international readership.

C23 Adachi, Ken. "This Author's Finally a Hero." *The Toronto Star*, 6 May 1978, p. D5.

Adachi calls *The Wars*, which has just won the Governor General's Award, "a literary work of art . . . a grippingly entertaining novel." The route to Findley's confirmation as one of Canada's "most original and important writers has been difficult and slow." Adachi describes Findley's acting career, his work for radio and television, and the writing of *The Wars*.

C24 "Perseverance Means Survival, Says Novelist after Award." *The Calgary Herald*, 1 June 1978, p. B14.

Winning the Governor General's Award proves ". . . you can survive if you persevere," says Findley. He recounts the difficulty he had getting his early novels published.

C25 Gilday, Katherine. "Writer Findley at Last Finds His Way in Out of the Cold." *The Globe and Mail* [Toronto], 22 July 1978, p. 29.

After the recent success of *The Wars*, Findley is still "star-struck by his sudden emergence into literary prominence." He is also diffident, a characteristic of both the man and the Southern Ontario culture that shaped him. Gilday finds evidence of Findley's scriptwriting experience in the "taut documentary-like structure and visual, highly dramatic quality of his fiction." Findley talks about the difficulty of writing scripts by committee and of the writer's paradox of having to be sensitive enough to create but tough enough to "bear the brunt of all the nasty, mean-minded things that are done to the products of your sensitivity." Findley also points out the joys of writing and of critical recognition. "Success doesn't solve any of your problems," he says, "but it does give you a certain kind of security . . . ."

C26 Bale, Doug. "Next Theatre London Play Revives Era of Macdonald." *The London Free Press*, 24 Jan. 1979, p. D9.

The next Theatre London play is *John A. — Himself!*. Findley wrote the play for William Hutt who played John A. Macdonald in CBC Television's *The National Dream*, scripted by Findley and William Whitehead. The "music-hall approach" was dictated by Findley's desire to make theatre more theatrical.

C27 Whittaker, Herbert. "Tim Findley Pursues the Playwright's Art." *The Globe and Mail* [Toronto], 16 Feb. 1979, p. 16.

Findley does not consider himself a "former novelist" even though he has two plays running at the moment. In fact, he feels he has to write a few more plays before he is satisfied with his achievement as a playwright. Findley recently talked to the director and actors after a performance of *Can You See Me Yet?* at Alumnae Theatre and praised the production for bringing out the play's fascist undertones and fire imagery. Findley comments on the criticism that his plays "take their time to come to terms with their audience." He is impatient with play workshopping and with playwrights who work out their experiences "in a small way." Findley has proven that he is a novelist of note, now ". . . he is out to prove himself equally gifted as a playwright."

C28 Kucherawy, Dennis. "Findley Discovers Awards Don't Guarantee Fame." *The London Free Press*, 17 Feb. 1979, p. B5.

This article profiles Findley's acting and writing careers. William Hutt is quoted as saying that Findley is an "imaginative and stunning story-teller." Findley expresses his concern with censorship, which he calls "intellectual blasphemy," and the lack of political freedom in Quebec.

C29 Kucherawy, Dennis. "Theatre Needs Artistic Identity." *The London Free Press*, 15 May 1979, p. A14.

Theatre London should produce more Canadian plays. Only one play in the 1978-79 season was an original Canadian script — Findley's *John A. — Himself!*.

C30 Casselman, William. "Give Up the Imitation American Dream Factory — We Have Ourselves to Observe." *Maclean's*, 28 May 1979, p. 51.

Casselman describes Findley's 15 years of writing television drama and talks to Findley about it. Findley calls working on *The Whiteoaks of Jalna* "a very unhappy experience" and says that the process of creation is the same whether he writes for theatre, film, or television, ". . . the character taps me on the shoulder and starts talking." He feels Canadian writers should not imitate American forms and "must learn that we have ourselves to observe." Casselman mistakenly credits Findley with scripting Centaur Theatre's production of *Piaf*.

C31 Cude, Wilfred. *A Due Sense of Differences: An Evaluative Approach to Canadian Literature*. Lanham, Md.: University Press of America, 1980, p. xvii.

The Wars is briefly mentioned in the Preface to this critical study of several Canadian novels. Cude praises Findley's technique, which "brilliantly plays realism and symbolism and myth against each other." He calls the novel "a polished accomplishment" that will endure with classics of imaginative reconstruction like Stephen Crane's *The Red Badge of Courage*.

C32 Rubin, Don, and Alison Cranmer-Byng. *Canada's Playwrights: A Biographical Guide*. Toronto: Canadian Theatre Review, 1980.

Biographical and bibliographical information with emphasis on writing for theatre, television, and radio.

C33 Cornell, Pamela. "Timothy Findley: Gentle Master of Violence." *The Graduate* [Univ. of Toronto], 7, No. 3 (Jan./Feb. 1980), 22, 24.

This article describes the career and work of the University of Toronto's new writer-in-residence. For Findley, violence is a creative force. He says, "I have a lot of violence inside me which is probably why I write about it so much." He comments on the craft of writing, his inspiration for *The Wars*, and education.

C34 Djwa, Sandra. "Deep Caves and Kitchen Linoleum: Psychological Violence in the Fiction of Alice Munro." In *Violence in the Canadian Novel since 1960/dans le roman canadien depuis 1960*. Ed. Virginia Harger-Grinling and Terry Goldie. [St. John's: Memorial Univ., 1981], p. 177.

The Wars is briefly mentioned as a novel whose violence reflects a "particular documentary framework."

C35 Jones, Joseph, and Johanna Jones. *Canadian Fiction*. Twayne's World Authors Series, No. 630. Boston: Twayne, 1981, pp. 85, 119.

In the chapter on humour, *The Butterfly Plague* is mentioned as an example of the wide range of subjects explored by Canadian humorists. In the chapter entitled "Searchers," Findley's fiction is discussed as an example of the "search for identity" variety. He "employs the novel to explore the theme of violence as the result of frustrated expectations."

C36 Kroetsch, Robert. "The Exploding Porcupine: Violence of Form in English-Canadian Fiction." In *Violence in the Canadian Novel since 1960 / dans le roman canadien depuis 1960*. Ed. Virginia Harger-Grinling and Terry Goldie. [St. John's: Memorial Univ., 1981], p. 191.

Kroetsch's essay, which first discusses violence in "classic" English-Canadian novels and then focuses on Michael Ondaatje's *Coming Through Slaughter*, mentions *The Wars* as a work that avoids violence. Robert Ross "lives ambiguously between the proofs and contradictions of his own experience of violence."

C37 Mathews, Robin. "Private Indulgence and Public Discipline: Violence in the English Canadian Novel Since 1960." In *Violence in the Canadian Novel since 1960 / dans le roman canadien depuis 1960*. Ed. Virginia Harger-Grinling and Terry Goldie. [St. John's: Memorial Univ., 1981], pp. 33-44.

Mathews examines physical violence in English-Canadian novels. He discusses novels of war, civil strife, corporate conflict, and self-indulgence, focusing on works by Findley and several other Canadian writers. While *The Wars* might be placed in the war novel category, it is really a "novel of self-indulgence" that portrays the civil world as decadent and the military world as pointless. The "heroes of war become the perplexed identity seekers who gain flashes of insight through moments of violence and erotic intensity." Mathews speculates that Findley's use of the phrase "floating through slaughter" connects his work, "whether by accident or design," to works by Leonard Cohen and Michael Ondaatje.

C38 Ricou, Laurie. "Obscured by Violence: Timothy Findley's *The Wars*." In *Violence in the Canadian Novel since 1960 / dans le roman canadien depuis 1960*. Ed. Virginia Harger-Grinling and Terry Goldie. [St. John's: Memorial Univ., 1981], pp. 125-37.

Before focusing on *The Wars*, Ricou discusses violence in Canadian literature in general and in war novels in particular. He finds in the latter that ". . . war has usually been distant incident and background." In contrast, Findley "describes the violent horror of war's incidents in excruciating detail" and draws the reader into contemplating the complex morality of violence and war by involving the reader in the same process of discovery undergone by the narrator. Findley suggests the possibility that ". . . violence obscures story, and story-teller, and even reader." The novel is not primarily the story of Robert Ross, but the extension of that story into the story of the narrator, and into the storymaking of the reader. The novel is a collage with photographs as a prominent device. Its short discrete sections, and short sentences and paragraphs give the effect of a series of snapshots. The phenomenon of "the mind stammering" in the face of violence is shared by Ross and the narrator. We must pay "special attention" to the narrator of this novel.

C39 Bilan, R.P. "End the Governor General Awards?". *The Canadian Forum*, June–July 1981, pp. 31-32.

Bilan questions some of the choices for the Governor General's Award for fiction. One poor decision was made in 1977 when *The Wars* received the award instead of Rudy Wiebe's *The Scorched-Wood People*. Canada's literary world is "very self-enclosed and incestuous." Margaret Atwood's rave review of *The Wars* and Findley's defence of Atwood after she received negative reviews of *Life Before Man* are examples of the "tightness" of the literary community.

C40 Amiel, Barbara. "Fiction's Brightest Season." *Maclean's*, 5 Oct. 1981, pp. 40-43.

This article on the 1981 fall book season and Canadian literature's "triumphant coming-of-age" calls *Famous Last Words* one of the season's "potential best sellers." Canadian writers are getting more attention and more money. Nancy Colbert, Findley's agent, is quoted as saying that Findley will receive about $250,000 for *The Wars* with subsidiary-rights sales. Findley, who now lives in "eclectic splendor in his Ontario farmhouse," has not forgotten the early days and finds it difficult to turn down any work.

C41 Blackadar, Bruce. "Findley and the Rise of Fascism." *The Toronto Star*, 22 Oct. 1981, p. F1.

During the four years it took Findley to write *Famous Last Words*, he came to realize that "Mauberley is in everyone, we're all fascists." Blackadar finds the novel "charged with sweeping historical insights, grand ironies, and enough riveting scenes to fill more than a few movies." Findley says that from dancing he learned timing and rhythm and from acting, pacing and nuance. Writing, he says, is "very hard work."

C42 Slopen, Beverley. "Findley and the Wordsmiths . . . Amnesty and Excellence." *Quill & Quire*, Nov. 1981, p. 17.
Slopen describes the four-year process of writing and editing *Famous Last Words*. Mauberley did not appear until two drafts had been completed. Few writers receive the kind of "nurturing" Findley received from editor John Pearce and publisher Bill Clarke.

C43 Adams, James. "From the Mind's Battlefield, a Vision of Rage — and Hope." *The Edmonton Journal*, 5 Dec. 1981, pp. D1, D4.
Adams' profile emphasizes Findley's recognition of life's "horrors," his anger at people's "willful ingenuousness," and his concern for the inhuman treatment of animals. Findley describes himself as "a very joyous person in a lot of ways," but his joy is born of suffering. Adams describes Findley's childhood, how he began to write, and his current works-in-progress.

C44 Kröller, Eva-Marie. "The Exploding Frame: Uses of Photography in Timothy Findley's *The Wars*." *Journal of Canadian Studies/Revue d'études canadiennes* [Trent Univ.], 16, Nos. 3-4 (Fall–Winter 1981), 68-74.
Kröller analyzes Findley's use of photography in *The Wars*. Photography is attractive to postmodernist writers both as metaphor and structural device because its "ambiguous function" exposes the limitations of any "prefabricated aesthetic order in rendering truth." Photographs strive to assert permanence but at the same time "strike at the root of cohesive, realist narrative and create a fragmented discourse with an unreliable or anonymous narrator." In such fictions attention is focused on the process rather than the product of photography in an effort to discover the moment at which the aesthetic frame encloses and diffuses experience. The primary function of photographs in *The Wars* is as "both object and means to the exposure of literary and political strategy." Kröller describes the structure of this novel as revolving around a series of experiences that imply a *camera obscura*. The ambiguous role of photography is summed up by a panel of stained glass, which, because it is out of context, is "a fragment whose full significance can only be guessed at." Likewise, the researcher attempts to piece together Robert Ross's life from fragments.

C45 Hulcoop, John F. " 'Look! Listen! Mark My Words!': Paying Attention to Timothy Findley's Fictions." *Canadian Literature*, No. 91 (Winter 1981), pp. 22-47.

Attention is crucial in understanding Findley's work. His writing compels the reader and critic to "pay attention" — to look, to listen, to mark his words by making direct appeals through sight, sound, and style. As well, "learning how and why we need to pay attention, is an important theme in all Findley's fictions." Hulcoop discusses instances of sight, sound, and style that demand the reader's attention in *Can You See Me Yet?*, "About Effie," "Harper's Bazaar," *The Last of the Crazy People*, *The Paper People*, *The Butterfly Plague*, "Hello Cheeverland, Goodbye," and *The Wars*. Insecurity, the search for identity, loneliness, waiting, nothingness, violent death, and especially fire are the recurring themes and events in Findley's work that demand our attention. The narrator instructs the reader how to pay attention, pulling our attention away from the "internal fiction" and making us refocus on the external relationship between reader and writer. Style is what makes the imagined world visible in Findley's work, "enabling us to see and therefore understand." Style also draws attention to the fact that we are reading fiction and reinforces his thematic concern with "the necessity of getting attention and the dangers of both getting and failing to get it." Hulcoop includes a Basic Checklist of Findley's work that lists some of his work for television.

C46 Klovan, Peter. " 'Bright and Good': Findley's 'The Wars.' " *Canadian Literature*, No. 91 (Winter 1981), pp. 58-69.

The Wars is an attempt to articulate the theme of how an individual transcends elemental forces even while he is being destroyed by them. The narrator has a tendency to view Robert Ross in naturalistic terms as a helpless child overwhelmed by a sinister world, but, at the same time, sees him as a tragic hero "who dares to challenge the dark necessity of his fate." The individual's isolation, nature viewed as a vast machine, identification with animals, and the pressures of heredity and environment are aspects of determinism that reinforce the novel's naturalism. The tension between naturalism and tragedy gives *The Wars* its "disturbing power, both as the poignant history of an individual, and as a metaphor of man's conflict with his fate." Klovan explores how the narrator resolves this dialectic. The narrator, "haunted by Robert's fiery sacrifice," comes to perceive his life as a tragic journey, marked by his progressive refinement and destruction by the elements of earth, water, air, and fire.

C47 New, W.H. "Beneath the Peaceable Kingdom." Editorial. *Canadian Literature*, No. 91 (Winter 1981), pp. 2-4.

New writes on several studies of Canadian literature including Virginia Harger-Grinling and Terry Goldie's *Violence in the Canadian Novel since 1960*. The essays in this collection explore the myth that Canada is "a peaceable kingdom" with "fiercer and more violent kingdoms" lying beneath the surface. New discusses essays by Robert Kroetsch (C36), Robin Mathews (C37), and Laurie Ricou (C38).

C48 Pirie, Bruce. "The Dragon in the Fog: 'Displaced Mythology' in 'The Wars.'" *Canadian Literature*, No. 91 (Winter 1981), pp. 70-79. Rpt. in *Contemporary Literary Criticism: Excerpts from Criticism of the Works of Today's Novelists, Poets, Playwrights, Short Story Writers, Filmmakers, and Other Creative Writers*. Ed. Jean C. Stine. Vol. xxvII. Detroit: Gale, 1984, 142-44.

Pirie describes *The Wars* as a "parody of romance" — a term used by Northrop Frye to denote the use of romantic mythical forms in material of realistic content. The novel's "almost documentary realism seems to seduce the reader into accepting the authenticity of the account," but verisimilitude is mixed with the "more truly seductive influence" of myth and legend. Many of the elements and themes of traditional romance can be found in *The Wars*: adventure, romantic love, a hero who begins in innocence and journeys in quest of knowledge, the union of human and animal identities, and a journey to the underworld. In this parody of romance, the hero quests to reintegrate his identity. Robert Ross achieves a kind of "fellow-feeling with nature" when he frees the horses. This life-giving act and its accompanying paradoxical life-taking are what Frye calls "a creatively negative act." Pirie concludes that the imaginative impact of *The Wars* comes from the romantic quest pattern, a pattern of which the casual reader may be unaware.

C49 Thompson, Eric. "Canadian Fiction of the Great War." *Canadian Literature*, No. 91 (Winter 1981), pp. 81-96.

Since publication of *The Wars*, readers have begun to realize that the war novel is a significant genre in Canadian fiction. Thompson discusses three novels about Canadian soldiers in World War I written between 1929 and 1937, as well as *The Wars*. Findley's novel is concerned with many of the same themes as the earlier works, but Findley presents the hero's conflicts of mind and spirit "in a more profound and convincing manner." Although the novel employs characteristic motifs, including "gritty" descriptions of battle, it goes further by creating an "enormously poignant drama of *personal heroism* in the midst of war." *The Wars* is also more successful in exploring the socio-cultural milieu of the war years. The novel's narrator acts as an archivist-interpreter, selecting and arranging, reconstructing the age and its people. The novel's bird and animal imagery, as well as several of its episodes and relationships, foreshadow and reinforce the "rising tide of violent passion" that leads to Robert Ross's "act of fury."

C50 Drolet, Gilbert. " 'Prayers Against Despair': A Retrospective Note on Findley's *The Wars.*" *Journal of Canadian Fiction*, No. 33 (1981-82), pp. 148-55.

Written five years after publication of *The Wars*, Drolet attempts "a more profound look" at the novel and its critical reception. One result of the power of Findley's style is the "intensity of recent criticism which tends to consider Robert Ross such an imposing literary creation that he transcends the fictional world . . . ." Findley's "extraordinary intuitiveness" allows him to approximate the reality of war as effectively as those who experienced it. To call Findley's work sentimental betrays a "fundamental misinterpretation of both the author's technique and purpose." Some critics have described *The Wars* as a romantic quest, seeing Ross's story as a journey from innocence to experience. Others have pointed out the naturalistic and tragic strains in the work, as well as the theme of the dehumanizing effect of war. Symbolism "unavoidably abounds" in a novel like *The Wars*; it contributes to the positive life-force evident throughout the novel.

C51 Cude, Wilfred. "Timothy Findley." In *Profiles in Canadian Literature*. Ed. Jeffrey M. Heath. Vol. iv. Toronto: Dundurn, 1982, 77-84.

Findley's writing covers a surprising range of genres. Cude briefly describes these and Findley's works, but concentrates on *The Wars*, "the author's most satisfying and most characteristic artistic statement thus far." The moral vision that informs the "terrible eloquence" of this novel leads Findley to expose the absolute finality of war through art rather than reality, through creativity rather than destruction. Findley achieves this by placing in suspension the distinctions between narrator and reader, narrator and character, and character and reader. The reader becomes one with the narrator, assembling Robert Ross's life to find its, and the novel's, meaning. *The Wars* chronicles the "shaping of a mature and intelligent adult who rejects . . . the madness of war." Findley has "dared to make clarity of statement his primary aesthetic objective." Cude includes a Chronology of Findley's life and work.

C52 MacFarlane, David. "The Perfect Gesture." *Books in Canada*, March 1982, pp. 5-8.
This profile is based on two conversations with Findley in which he talked about his life and work, particularly about the writing of *The Wars* and *Famous Last Words*. Many of the details for *The Wars* came from the letters of an uncle who died of war injuries. Unlike *The Wars*, with *Famous Last Words* he experienced no "moment of recognition." Its writing and editing were long and gruelling, and Findley still wonders if the novel was "given to the wrong person." He believes you never learn how to write; "every time you sit down you learn it all over again." Findley also describes the writing and reception of his early novels, noting that there were only two Canadian reviews of *The Butterfly Plague*. He tells MacFarlane the "overriding image of my life, [is] that we are here for the slaughter." Findley turned to the theatre seeking "the perfection of gesture" he had found in dance, a career he was unable to pursue.

C53 Metcalf, John. *Kicking Against the Pricks*. Downsview: ECW, 1982, p. 124. Rpt. in *Kicking Against the Pricks*. Guelph, Ont.: Red Kite, 1986, p. 124.
Metcalf relates how he chaired a committee, made up of Margaret Laurence, Alice Munro, Fred Bodsworth, and Findley responsible for drawing up membership criteria for the Writers' Union of Canada.

C54 Widerman, Jane. "New Protection for the Author: Libel Insurance." *Maclean's*, 16 Aug. 1982, p. 46.
Authors' insurance is becoming popular among Canadian writers. Before publication of *Famous Last Words* in the United States, Findley insured himself against slander, libel, and invasion of privacy charges. The potential threat comes from the Duchess of Windsor, who has a reputation for suing publishers.

C55 McIver, Jack. "Timothy Findley's Private Wars." *Quest*, Oct. 1982, pp. 76-78, 80-83.

Recognition has finally come to a writer who has "paid for it in full." McIver visited Findley at his farm near Cannington, Ontario and describes the house, the pets, and Findley and William Whitehead's life there. Findley's mind is charged with the "touchstones of past injustices or cruelties," and a "part of him seems almost *wired* to the past." Combined with his faculty for detail and sense of drama, these features inspire his writing. McIver describes Findley's self-doubt as his "personal undertoad . . . threatening to pull him down, and if not destroy him, silence him for good." Findley says that for him New York in the 1960s and 1970s was "the ultimate horror place" and relates some of his experiences there. McIver includes comments on Findley and his work from his agent, Nancy Colbert, and his editor, John Pearce.

C56 MacGregor, Roy. "Who Killed Sir Harry?". *Books in Canada*, Nov. 1982, pp. 6-8.

MacGregor describes the life and unsolved murder of Sir Harry Oakes, about which there is much written speculation. *Famous Last Words* continues this tradition in a fictional format. It connects Oakes's murder with the rumoured Nazi sympathies of the Duke and Duchess of Windsor. Findley notes that "writers aren't just busybodies." His concern with the spread of fascism brought him to Oakes's story.

C57 Strong, Joanne. "The Informal Timothy Findley." *The Globe and Mail* [Toronto], 20 Nov. 1982, "Entertainment," p. 14.

Strong describes Findley's preference for life in the country. She relates how Findley's writing career began and the people who helped him. Findley comments that writing is hard work and that he reads aloud everything he writes.

C58 New, W.H. Introduction. "Canada." *Journal of Commonwealth Literature* [London], 17, No. 2 (Dec. 1982), 52.

New reviews Canadian literature for 1981. Of the many fall releases, Mavis Gallant's *Home Truths* and Findley's *Famous Last Words* received the most critical attention. Both are "substantial works of fiction," and both encapsulate several of the year's recurrent patterns: a tension between the familiar and the foreign, an increased consciousness of other parts of the Commonwealth, a use of documentary as part of other genres, and an exploration of ritualistic impulses. *Famous Last Words* is the more theatrical of the two novels, and it "draws more overt attention to its own processes of approximation." It is "meant to be read as comments on the sources of violence, not merely as fictional entertainments."

C59 Coldwell, Joan. "Findley, Timothy." *The Oxford Companion to Canadian Literature.* Ed. William Toye. Toronto: Oxford Univ. Press, 1983.

The entry includes biographical information, a short list of critical sources, and comments on Findley's novels (up to and including *Famous Last Words*), the play *Can You See Me Yet?*, and his work for radio and television. Findley's fiction uses metaphors and structural devices from the medium of film. Madness, violence, and fascism are found in all of his work. Coldwell concludes that the paradox at the heart of Findley's fictional world is that "in an insane world an act of violence may be the only sane response: an act of love."

C60 Hoy, Helen. "Findley, Timothy (1930–   )." *Modern English-Canadian Prose: A Guide to Information Sources.* American Literature, English Literature, and World Literature in English Information Guide Series. Vol. xxxviii. Detroit: Gale, 1983.

Findley's early work and *The Wars* are described as having a "surreal quality" and as exploring "the issue of emotional integrity in prose that is fresh and precise." Hoy includes a brief bibliography of primary and secondary material and biographical information.

C61 Miller, Mary Jane. "An Analysis of *The Paper People.*" *Canadian Drama/L'Art dramatique canadien* [Univ. of Waterloo], 9 (1983), 49-62.

In the same issue in which the script of *The Paper People* is published (B21), Miller offers an analysis sixteen years after the television play was first broadcast. She calls it "one of the most innovative television dramas" in the *Festival* series and notes that critics either loved it or hated it. It is "an articulate message" from young Canadian artists to a "self-satisfied, 'expo-centered' majority." As well as "a cutting glance" at our documentary tradition, a comment on our lack of flair for self-dramatization, and an exploration of the despair of Canadian artists in the 1960s, the film outlines our cultural history and gives "fresh urgency to still unresolved questions about Canada's identity." Miller describes the film's two plot lines, its film-within-a-film structure, and its documentary techniques. The film's highly stylized mode is in tension with television's naturalism. Miller also discusses changes made in the script for the final production. The film is important as social history, as an early example of Findley's work, and as "a carefully crafted narrative."

C62 Marchand, Philip. "Timothy Findley: Novelist on a High Wire." *Chatelaine*, Feb. 1983, pp. 44, 96, 98, 100.
Marchand calls Findley's life "one of the most tormented — and extraordinary — lives led by a major Canadian writer." This profile covers Findley's childhood and his acting and writing careers. His childhood was characterized by strong women, an absent father, the presence of death, and loneliness. Marchand quotes William Hutt who calls William Whitehead Findley's godsend: "Bill's loyalty and care and concern have . . . contributed to Tiff's being able to achieve what he's achieved."

C63 Gervais, Marty. "Writing and the Writer." *The Windsor Star*, 26 Feb. 1983, "On Books," p. C10.
Gervais describes Findley at a reading at Wayne State University and their conversation about his writing. Findley regards his writing as "a process of exploration" and says he is still learning. He comments on critics who try to second-guess a writer and describes his own writing methods. He stresses the importance of reading his work aloud: "If you can't read something out loud, then you can't read it in your mind."

C64 F., J. "The Sound of Writers Reading." *The Globe and Mail* [Toronto], 28 May 1983, "Fanfare," p. 2.
Several Canadian writers relate their experiences doing public readings to promote their books. Findley tells of a reading at a small college which only five students attended, three who obviously had been told to come and two who wandered in by mistake. During a reading he works at reaching the audience, doing justice to his work, and presenting the work in the proper voice. Although Findley does not mind readings, he does not like to "flog" his books.

C65 Vauthier, Simone. "Photo-Roman: *The Wars* de Timothy Findley." *Études canadiennes/Canadian Studies* [Univ. de Bordeaux III], No. 14 (June/ juin 1983), pp. 101-19.
When Findley gave photographs an eminent place in *The Wars*, he was following in a long tradition of writers who have been interested in photography. Vauthier examines the function of photographs as objects in Findley's novel. If a novelist is "un parleur d'objets," then

Findley is as much a "teller" of photographs as he is a "teller" of war. Photographs occupy an important place in novels like *The Wars* that see themselves as historical, since they will always be torn between the poles of the factual reference and that of the fiction. Vauthier identifies three narrative voices in the novel: the researcher, the narrator, and the writer. She examines photographs in the novel not as representations of absent objects but for what they give to us themselves, "des images du monde," which have their own story. If we can see in Robert Ross a mirror of our own violence, innocence, and death, then *The Wars* can be, like a photograph, "un instrument de vie." In French.

C66 Fitzgerald, Judith. "From *The Wars* to a Blind Cat on the Ark." *The Globe and Mail* [Toronto], 2 July 1983, "Entertainment," p. 3.

Fitzgerald visited Findley at his farm near Cannington, Ontario and reports on their conversation as well as outlining his writing career. She describes Findley's house, relates the story of the stone wall, and quotes Robert Weaver's admiration for Findley and his work. William Whitehead calls himself Findley's "first editor" and describes how the novelist tends to get "stopped at walls and doors in his work." Findley discusses his new book, *Not Wanted on the Voyage*, which he says has to do with the covenant and Arnold Toynbee's theory about the consequences of having chosen one God. Findley describes his former alcoholism and says homosexuality has never been an issue with either him or Whitehead. They are accepted in Cannington as "the boys." Findley also talks about his fear that other writers will use his ideas, about how he has been misinterpreted, and about a writer's responsibility in society.

C67 Moon, Barbara. "Fixing the Books." *Saturday Night*, Aug. 1983, pp. 55-58.

In this article about Canadian best-seller lists, Moon mentions *Famous Last Words* as an example of a book that fared quite differently on the *Maclean's* and *Toronto Star* lists. Findley was one of the first to benefit from a publisher's bonus given to an author whose book appears on both best-seller lists.

C68 Heward, Burt. "Findley Finds Inspiration in Peaceful Country Life." *The Citizen* [Ottawa], 12 Aug. 1983, p. 58.

Heward focuses on Findley's farm near Cannington and his life there with Whitehead and their many pets. He also describes Findley's childhood, acting career, and drinking problem. Findley is working on

Not Wanted on the Voyage, and Heward discusses the beginnings of this work.

C69 Gloin, Lew. "Findley Novel Revived." *The Toronto Star*, 4 Sept. 1983, "Books," p. G6.
The Last of the Crazy People has been republished in paperback. Like *The Butterfly Plague*, it was originally rejected by Canadian publishers. Gloin speculates that the novel's Toronto setting is what has kept it from getting critical attention: ". . . everyone knows nothing ever happens *there*."

C70 "Cannington" and "Kirkland Lake." *Canadian Literary Landmarks*. Ed. John Robert Colombo. Willowdale, Ont.: Hounslow, 1984, pp. 112, 130.
Cannington, "a farm community east of Lake Simcoe," is listed as Findley's home since 1964. The entry for Kirkland Lake notes its association with Sir Harry Oakes, a character in *Famous Last Words*.

C71 "Findley, Timothy 1930– ." *Contemporary Authors: A Bio-Bibliographic Guide to Current Writers in Fiction, General Non-Fiction, Poetry, Journalism, Drama, Motion Pictures, Television, and Other Fields*. New Revision. Ed. Linda Metzger. Vol. XII. Detroit: Gale, 1984.
Includes biographical information, lists of publications and awards, as well as excerpts from interviews and critical articles about his work.

C72 Howells, Coral Ann. " 'History as She is Never Writ': *The Wars* and *Famous Last Words*." *Kunapipi* [Aarhus, Denmark], 6, No. 1 (1984), 49-56.
The Wars and *Famous Last Words* are historical novels; they are also stories about writing and reading. Both novels "problematise" history since they "blur the distinctions between referential fact and interpretive fiction." Howell's essay explores the "literariness" of Findley's fictions, the enigmas he pursues, and his creative invention using other literary works. These texts refer both to history and to other fictions. The protagonists' names are the most important referents. Robert Ross was Oscar Wilde's Canadian lover who collaborated with him on *Portrait of Mr W.H.* Howells points to many similarities between Wilde's fiction and *The Wars*. Hugh Selwyn Mauberley has a more obvious referent as the character of Ezra Pound's poem. As well as many echoes of the poem, Findley's text "has appropriated Pound's images and literalised

his metaphors . . . ." As a work about writing and reading, *Famous Last Words* focuses on the play between determinism (historical fact) and the assertion of free will (the choice of fictive elements). The emphasis falls not on truth but on interpretation.

C73   Hutcheon, Linda. "The 'Postmodernist' Scribe: The Dynamic Stasis of Contemporary Canadian Writing." *University of Toronto Quarterly*, 53 (Spring 1984), 284, 286-87, 290, 293. Rpt. (revised) in *The Canadian Postmodern: A Study of Contemporary English-Canadian Fiction.* By Linda Hutcheon. Toronto: Oxford Univ. Press, 1988, pp. 45-60.

Hutcheon explores the question of why so many Canadian writers have used the taking and viewing of photographs as an analogy for literary production. Such an analogy suggests that writing fiction is "an act of petrifying into stasis the dynamics of experience." In her study of several Canadian postmodern novels, Hutcheon discovers that there is also "a resurrecting process" — the positive act of reading. In *The Wars*, Findley uses transcripts of tape-recorded interviews with imaginary characters and descriptions of photographs to create "a double distance." These devices are problematic in that while they record, they also frame and "automatize" experience. These media must be activated by the reader, in order to reverse the process and "resurrect that creative immediacy" lost in the process of fixing experience.

C74   Kröller, Eva-Marie. "The Eye in the Text: Timothy Findley's *The Last of the Crazy People* and Alice Munro's *Lives of Girls and Women.*" *World Literature Written in English* [Univ. of Guelph], 23, No. 2 (Spring 1984), 366-74.

Although *The Last of the Crazy People* and Alice Munro's *Lives of Girls and Women* have been classified as realistic novels, Kröller suggests that they can also be read as metafiction, as "writing reflecting on its own premises." The focus of both texts is on the "I/eye" of the adolescent protagonists. Their perceptions form "a series of textual levels" that both support and undermine the text's mimetic surface. Photography, television, and especially the human eye function as *camera obscura* in these novels. Del's and Hooker's perceptions establish the basis for the novel's "architexture" — "the combination of structure and texture visible in a given work." The protagonists' rites of passage are duplicated as the reader absorbs the text and penetrates its structure in his or her own attempts at "crossing the threshold to the novel." Kröller points out several elements in Findley's novel, including closed doors, smoke, silence, masks, and repetition, which reinforce the idea that language can be a refusal to acknowledge reality while, at the same time, exposing "the flimsy fabric of artifact." The "opacity" of these novels' realistic surface is made transparent through the children's eyes. The reader, in the act of reading, parallels this experience.

C75 Miller, Mary Jane. "Canadian Television Drama 1952-1970: Canada's National Theatre." *Theatre History in Canada*, 5, No. 1 (Spring 1984), 51-71.

Miller proposes that from the mid-1950s to 1970 television drama served as Canada's national theatre and fostered the growth of Canadian dramatic arts. Television created an outlet for many Canadian writers. Findley wrote scripts for *The National Dream*, *The Whiteoaks of Jalna*, and *The Newcomers* series. His controversial television drama, *The Paper People*, is a "superbly original" work, one of only a few commissioned Canadian plays produced between 1952 and 1970.

C76 Manguel, Alberto. "You Must Read These Books." *The Globe and Mail* [Toronto], 21 April 1984, "Books," p. 7.

Manguel asks ten Canadian writers to recommend little-read Canadian books. Findley chooses Scott Symons' *Place d'Armes*, Dennis Lee's *The Gods*, and Marian Engel's *The Honeyman Festival*.

C77 Streeter, Jim. "Canadian Literature Still Goes Unrecognized." Letter. *The Toronto Star*, 25 May 1984, p. A16.

Streeter's letter refuting an article stating that Canadian universities ignore Canadian literature, mentions Findley as a writer who has provided "a mirror" that has helped shape our imaginative vision.

C78 Livesay, Dorothy. "The Canadian Documentary: An Overview." Long-liners Conference on the Canadian Long Poem, Calumet College, York Univ., Toronto. 29 May–1 June 1984. Printed in *Open Letter* [Long-liners Conference Issue], Ser. 6, Nos. 2-3 (Summer–Fall 1985), p. 127.

The Wars is an example of the genre of the long poem — "an archive for our time" — that is dramatic, documentary, and relevant. "Written as a novel but powerfully vivid when presented on the screen," the work is "a fusion of dialogue and imagery."

C79 Scobie, Stephen. "I and I: Phyllis Webb's 'I Daniel.' " Long-liners Conference on the Canadian Long Poem, Calumet College, York Univ., Toronto. 29 May–1 June 1984. Printed in *Open Letter* [Long-liners Conference Issue], Ser. 6, Nos. 2-3 (Summer–Fall 1985), pp. 62-64, 66.

Scobie writes on the prevalence of the documentary form in Canadian literature, equating documentary to "a question of identity." Mirrors are a pervasive image in documentary works and "one of its most extravagant and bravura occurrences" is found in *Famous Last Words* when the Duke crashes through his mirror image. The use of Ezra Pound's Mauberley, references to the Book of Daniel, and mirror imagery make this novel an "intertextual" double to Phyllis Webb's poem "I, Daniel." Webb dedicated the poem to Findley (C204) and Findley dedicated *Famous Last Words* to her.

C80 Adachi, Ken. "Book Show a Noble but Failed Experiment." *The Toronto Star*, 25 June 1984, "Books," p. C2.

In an article on the Canadian Booksellers Association show ("people stayed away in droves") and convention ("the mood was upbeat"), Adachi mentions that Findley was honoured as Author of the Year.

C81 Good, Cynthia. "Awards Banquet: Author of the Year." *Canadian Bookseller*, June–July 1984, p. 26.

A condensed version of C82.

C82 Good, Cynthia. "Timothy Findley: Author of the Year." *Canadian Bookseller*, June–July 1984, p. 12.

Good describes Findley's acting career and his change to writing. Findley says he misses the theatre world, but not the acting. She briefly summarizes his novels and comments that his "unconventional punctuation" reinforces the "dramatic aspect" of his work by almost forcing the reader to read aloud.

C83 Abley, Mark. "The Master Storytellers." *Maclean's*, 23 July 1984, p. 47.

Dinner Along the Amazon is the "jewel" among the four initial titles in Penguin's new Short Fiction series. Findley's first collection of short stories "reveals the passionate intelligence of a major artist."

C84 "Findley, Stevenson Novels Named Best Paperbacks." *The Toronto Star*, 30 Oct. 1984, p. H3.

The Last of the Crazy People is one of two novels named the best English-language paperbacks for 1984 at the Periodical Distributors of Canada awards banquet.

C85 "Findley Wins Author's Award." *The Globe and Mail* [Toronto], 30 Oct. 1984, "Entertainment," p. M7.
The Last of the Crazy People has won the Author's Award for paperback fiction sponsored by the Foundation for the Advancement of Canadian Letters and the Periodical Distributors of Canada.

C86 "Findley Wins Author's Award." *The Chronicle-Herald* [Halifax], 31 Oct. 1984, p. E2.
The Last of the Crazy People has been named best English-language fiction paperback for 1984.

C87 Howells, Coral Ann. " 'Tis Sixty Years Since': Timothy Findley's *The Wars* and Roger McDonald's *1915*." *World Literature Written in English* [Univ. of Guelph], 23 (Winter 1984), 129-36.
Howells attempts to situate *The Wars* and Australian Roger McDonald's *1915* in the tradition of World War I novels and discovers how they "transform history into myths with distinctively national colouring." Both writers are interested in the pattern of history as it affects the individual and the human species. Both rewrite history through the medium of other writing about the war. Although Findley's novel is not overtly nationalistic, the name of his protagonist makes him distinctly Canadian. That it is a Canadian hero who "affirms the universal humanist values" demonstrates "a proper sense of national spirit." Robert Ross's acts of disobedience read very differently sixty years later, "freed from the prison of their historical moment."

C88 Staines, David. "Montreal Holds Special Memories for Award-Winning Writer." *The Gazette* [Montreal], 10 Nov. 1984, p. I1.
Staines writes of Findley's visit to Montreal to receive the Author's Award and comments on Findley's associations with that city. Findley met Marie-Claire Blais, a writer for whom he has "immense admiration and great love," in Montreal. Findley comments that Montrealers have the gift of "being oneself." He discusses the writing of *Not Wanted on the Voyage*, his blind cat Mottyl who inspired its beginnings, and the Phyllis Webb poem that influenced its direction. Findley says that a

49

writer must watch society, stand guard, and speak out: "Writing is the articulation of the things that must be said."

C89 Marck, James. "Findley's Right Fight." *Now* [Toronto], 29 Nov.– 5 Dec. 1984, p. 9.

Based on a talk with Findley shortly after publication of *Not Wanted on the Voyage*, Marck writes about that novel and Findley's political and social views. The novel is "all about the blurring of the conventional lines of good and evil." Findley does not consider himself a satirist, but as an allegorical fable, *Not Wanted on the Voyage* "comes pretty close to satire." George Orwell's *Animal Farm* was a "loose model" for the novel. Findley believes that an artist has "an obligation to raise his voice in opposition to militarism and hegemony . . . ." He feels that we are living in "inutterably dangerous times."

C90 Burns, K. "Findley Needs New Act." Letter. *Now* [Toronto], 13-19 Dec. 1984, p. 4.

Responding to James Marck's article (C89), Burns is highly critical of Findley, his work, and Marck's article.

C91 Duffy, Dennis. "Let Us Compare Histories: Meaning and Mythology in Findley's *Famous Last Words*." *Essays on Canadian Writing* [10th Anniversary Issue], No. 30 (Winter 1984-85), pp. 187-205.

Duffy attempts to locate and define exactly what gives *Famous Last Words* its power and authority. The novel is a postmodernist fiction that "deals with the beholder's response to the spectacular corruption of a figure who ought to have been a hero." The genesis of this novel's political and social setting can be found in *The Butterfly Plague*, and its play with narrative technique originates in *The Wars*. *Famous Last Words* heightens this narrative play, calling attention to itself and to the fact that it is "made-up, planned, imposed upon a wealth of events." Duffy demonstrates how Findley uses the Windsors to convey both stylistically and thematically his view of the interpenetration of fact and fiction, of history and mythology. He also analyzes Mauberley's role and the effect of his narrative in destroying one myth of aesthetic perception and setting another in its place. "*Famous Last Words* may combine the temporal setting of *The Butterfly Plague* with the narrative play of *The Wars*, but it conveys a message all its own, one easily overlooked in our amazement at the novel's technique."

C92 Hutcheon, Linda. "Canadian Historiographic Metafiction." *Essays on Canadian Writing* [10th Anniversary Issue], No. 30 (Winter 1984-85), pp. 229-30, 231, 235. Rpt. (revised "Historiographic Metafiction") in *The Canadian Postmodern: A Study of Contemporary English-Canadian Fiction*. By Linda Hutcheon. Toronto: Oxford Univ. Press, 1988, pp. 61-77.

Hutcheon discusses the process of *énonciation* — the joint creative acts of writing and reading — in recent Canadian historiographic metafiction. In *Famous Last Words*, Mauberley, the producer of the text-within-the-text, represents the artist as aesthete who is only a voyeur. The reader is also a voyeur "whose vision of the hero's text . . . is literally controlled by another character," Quinn. As voyeurs, we cannot be exempt from the "implications of the novel's moral theme of silence and the responsibility of action." Because this type of metafiction "thematizes its own interaction both with the historical past and with the historically conditioned expectations of its readers . . . the reader becomes the actualizing link between history and fiction."

C93 Scobie, Stephen. "Eye-Deep in Hell: Ezra Pound, Timothy Findley, and Hugh Selwyn Mauberley." *Essays on Canadian Writing* [10th Anniversary Issue], No. 30 (Winter 1984– 85), pp. 206-27.

Scobie's essay explores Findley's use of Ezra Pound's character in *Famous Last Words*. Findley's references to Pound's poem are thorough and complex but its exact status in Findley's fictional world is uncertain. His characterization of Mauberley "obviously, and quite properly, diverges drastically from Pound's," but there are some similarities. Above all, both "exemplify and bear witness to the aesthetic, emotional, political, and moral failures of their times." What distinguishes Findley's Mauberley is the greater strength, thoroughness, and heroism of his bearing witness. Mauberley's heroism is his "capacity to express a clear-sighted vision of his moral position." Scobie sees that position as one of "humiliation," which explains Mauberley's attraction to fascism. Findley presents Mauberley's attempts at "clear demarcation" in terms of two distortions of visual perception: vision as seen in a mirror and vision as seen through one eye. Scobie describes several instances of both of these effects.

C94 Booth, James, Susheila Nasta, and Owen Knowles. "African, Caribbean, and Canadian Literature." In *The Year's Work in English*

Studies. Ed. Laurel Brake. Vol. LXIII. Atlantic Highlands, N.J.: Humanities, 1985, 490.

In this review of critical work in English studies, the authors mention two articles published in *Journal of Canadian Fiction*: Johan Aitken's interview (C185) and Gilbert Drolet's essay on *The Wars* (C50).

C95 Duffy, Dennis. "The Rejection of Modernity in Recent Canadian Fiction." *Canadian Issues/Thèmes canadiens*, 7 (1985), 260-73.

Leonard Cohen's *Beautiful Losers* demonstrated that the age of literary modernism in Canada was over. *The Wars*, Margaret Atwood's *Surfacing*, and Marian Engel's *Bear* continue the theme of *Beautiful Losers* "and perhaps extend it." These novels reject modern culture and try to "locate a new grounding for the self." They do not, however, move beyond lamentations and leave the individual "no genuine alternative to that of solitude." The novels share an atmosphere of mystery, clearly defined sets of oppositions, and a loveless sexuality. The ending of *The Wars* is the most complex of the novels' weak endings but is scarcely "a fitting solution to the cultural crises that the novel has depicted."

C96 Hutcheon, Linda. *A Theory of Parody: The Teachings of Twentieth-Century Art Forms*. New York: Methuen, 1985, pp. 35, 111, 115.

Hutcheon's book is a study of parody, of "the implications for theory of modern artistic practice." Parody is an important mode of self-reflexivity in literature for writers like Findley. Hutcheon discusses Ezra Pound's Mauberley as existing in an ironic inversion of the aesthetic and moral world of Dante's *Divine Comedy*. Findley's use of the Pound text as the parodic background of *Famous Last Words* "adds another level of complexity to the ideological function of parody." She notes that we cannot separate parody and history in this novel, nor ignore its ideological commentary on the silence of aestheticism. Parody can also have the power to renew, and clearly, in *Famous Last Words*, this renewal can have social implications.

C97 Keith, W.J. *Canadian Literature in English*. Longman Literature in English. London: Longman, 1985, pp. 170, 251.

In chapter ix, "Creating Fictional Worlds of Wonder," Keith discusses contemporary writers who have built out of their Canadian experience "an exciting if sometimes disturbing variety of imaginative worlds of wonder." Findley is a "magical melodramatist" and Keith briefly discusses Findley's first four novels as "intellectual melodrama." Their "almost paranoiac intensity" is both "impressive and disturbing." Keith lists Findley's major works and two critical articles in a brief bibliography.

C98 McGregor, Gaile. *The Wacousta Syndrome: Explorations in the Canadian Langscape*. Toronto: Univ. of Toronto Press, 1985, pp. 80, 89-90, 106-07, 109, 114, 117, 123-24, 130, 138, 184-86, 195-96, 287, 320, 370, 399-400, 407, 424, 428, 441.

What McGregor calls the Wacousta Syndrome, "a recoil from nature," has served as background to the Canadian sense of self. McGregor explores the iconography that has expressed this syndrome and some of the features of the fictional worlds that have been constructed on its foundation. McGregor discusses *The Last of the Crazy People*, *The Butterfly Plague*, and *The Wars* throughout her book. She identifies in Findley's work several features of the Wacousta Syndrome including nightmare vision, fog imagery, the theme of isolation, an obsession with death, war which isolates men, determinism, women as sexual predators, vulnerable children, animals identified with self, involvement of the reader in the work, a Jungian approach to the psyche, and the use of photography as metaphor.

C99 Vauthier, Simone. "The Dubious Battle of Storytelling: Narrative Strategies in Timothy Findley's *The Wars*." In *Gaining Ground: European Critics on Canadian Literature*. Ed. Robert Kroetsch and Reingard M. Nischik. Western Canadian Literary Documents. Vol. VI. Edmonton: NeWest, 1985, 11-39.

The Wars asserts the authority of the novelist while questioning the adequacy of narrative "to come to grips with the stark and obscene realities of war." Vauthier's essay surveys some of the strategies by which narrative authority is achieved and/or undermined. The basic fictional premise of this novel is that the story of Robert Ross needs to be "rescued from oblivion, since it has been obscured by the quiet violence of silence." Vauthier identifies three narrative voices in *The Wars*: the first person "I-narrator," the second person "you-researcher," and the "scriptor . . . the arranger of collocations." She explores how the authority of each of these voices is achieved and how it is undermined in the text. The narrative strands are held together by the scriptor, but like the narrator, he is unable to weave a continuous story out of the fragments. This failure sends the reader back to the author, "the creator of this alternative world which has been presented as part of the real world."

C100 Woodcock, George. "History to the Defeated: Notes on Some Novels by Timothy Findley." In *The Canadian Novel*. Ed. John Moss. Vol IV. Toronto: NC, 1985, 15-28. Rpt. (revised and expanded — "History to the Defeated: Some Fictions of Timothy Findley") in *Northern Spring: The Flowering of Canadian Literature*. By George Woodcock. Vancouver: Douglas & McIntyre, 1987, pp. 159-77.

Findley not only shares an historic consciousness with Canadian writers of his generation, he is also, in a more specific sense, an historical novelist. He reshapes events for aesthetic purposes so that his novels stand as literary artifacts outside their historical context. Woodcock discusses *The Wars*, *Famous Last Words*, and, in *Northern Spring*, *Not Wanted on the Voyage*. Robert Ross and Mauberley are both, by normal standards, utterly defeated. History can neither help nor pardon them, but literature offers understanding and compassion. In *The Wars*, Ross's retention of his humanity is his triumph. The elements and the relationship between men and animals play significant symbolic and formal roles in the novel. In *Famous Last Words*, Findley mixes characters from literature and history to create a work that "acknowledges no myths but its own." Mauberley is both a weak man and an "artist who feels a complete power over what he creates." In this novel, Findley presents his views "on the nature and effects of war and the real character of history." *Not Wanted on the Voyage* is less a revision of history than "the remythologization of a myth." The novel expresses a Gnostic view of the natural order and the nature of God. Like Findley's earliest novels, it ends "with the defiance of actual history," which because it is the "chronicle of multiple deaths," must be reconstructed.

C101 Cameron, Elspeth. "The Inner Wars of Timothy Findley." *Saturday Night*, Jan. 1985, pp. 24-33.

Cameron suggests that Findley's life and art have been shaped by childhood experiences with separation anxiety, illness and death, loneliness, and a sense of abandonment. These early experiences led at times to self-destructive bouts of self-pity and drinking but, at other times, "his fears spurred extraordinary creativity." His search for "a perfect creative outlet" led him to false starts in ballet, acting, and playwriting. Cameron describes each member of Findley's "sensitive, imaginative"

Rosedale family. Findley has called childhood "unmitigated *hell* from beginning to end." He hated boarding school and missed much of his later schooling due to real and "enhanced" illnesses. Cameron details Findley's acting experience, the people who led him to writing, his brief marriage, and his partnership with William Whitehead, "a man of extraordinary gifts." She describes the writing, publication, and critical reception of his first four novels. Findley became disillusioned with artistic collaboration following the production of two of his films and was angered that his early novels were ignored in his own country. Findley now "sees his life as the ideal preparation for writing."

C102 Noonan, James. "The National Arts Centre: Fifteen Years at Play." *Theatre History in Canada*, 6, No. 1 (Spring 1985), 56-81.

Noonan reviews the history of English and French theatre at the National Arts Centre in Ottawa. He quotes from a National Arts Centre *Annual Report* (C10) announcing Findley's appointment at the Centre as the first playwright-in-residence and their intention to produce his play, *Can You See Me Yet?*. Noonan sees this as "a new dimension of its involvement in Canadian theatre, the development of new Canadian plays."

C103 Adachi, Ken. "Translated Czech Novel in Race for Top Literary Prize." *The Toronto Star*, 16 May 1985, p. E3.

Not Wanted on the Voyage is one of four contenders for the Governor General's Award for English-language fiction.

C104 French, William. "Finalists Named for Book Awards." *The Globe and Mail* [Toronto], 16 May 1985, "Entertainment," p. E1.

Not Wanted on the Voyage has been nominated for the Governor General's Award for English-language fiction.

C105 "Findley and Cohen Win Literary Award." *The Globe and Mail* [Toronto], 23 May 1985, "Entertainment," p. E5.

Not Wanted on the Voyage has won the Canadian Authors Association literary award for best novel.

C106 "Findley Awarded Top Prize for Best Fiction." *The Toronto Star*, 23 May 1985, p. H3.

Not Wanted on the Voyage has won the Canadian Authors Association award for best fiction. The judges said that ". . . it both respects the conventions of the novel and transcends them."

C107 "Findley, Cohen Win $5000 Each in Contest." *The London Free Press*, 23 May 1985, p. D5.

Not Wanted on the Voyage is one of two books "with religious themes" to win the 1985 Canadian Authors Association literary award.

C108 York, Lorraine M. " 'A Shout of Recognition': 'Likeness' and the Art of the Simile in Timothy Findley's *The Wars*." *English Studies in Canada*, 11 (June 1985), 223-30.

York writes that the simile is "deftly manipulated" by Findley to impress upon his readers the "bewildering interplay between horrific and ordinary experience, and individual and collective tragedy which lies at the very heart of every war." Findley uses similes to "defamiliarize" ordinary experience in the scenes before Robert Ross goes to the front to suggest the horrors of war. He also uses them to "familiarize" the war experience by forcing them into the framework of the ordinary past. Similes of this last type include those involving sports, childhood fantasy, and animals. York suggests and discusses several examples of each of these.

C109 "Writer-in-Residence." *Winnipeg Free Press*, 4 Oct. 1985, p. 31.

Findley has been appointed writer-in-residence at the University of Winnipeg, but for only two weeks. It is difficult to get funding for such programmes.

C110 McWhirter, George. "Creativity at UBC." Letter. *The Globe and Mail* [Toronto], 3 Dec. 1985, p. A7.

In response to an article on creative writing in Canadian universities, McWhirter describes Findley as a writer "who can handle livestock (animal and human) as intricately in barnyards and battlefields as Jane Austen in her drawing rooms, but not like Hemingway with rod and gun in his belt . . . ."

See C123.

C111 Twiston-Davies, David. "A New Image for Canadians." *The Globe and Mail* [Toronto], 14 Dec. 1985, Books: Literary Supp., p. E5.

It has been a good year for Canadian literature in Britain. Twiston-Davies writes from London about bookselling and promotion, Canadian studies programmes, and literary awards. Findley's recent public reading was "the greatest pleasure to hear," and *Not Wanted on the*

Voyage is receiving praise for its "witty observation" and "assured" handling of the Noah's ark theme.

C112 MacLeod, Hilary. "Timothy Findley Writes for Peace." *The Canadian Author & Bookman*, 61, No. 2 (Winter 1985), 3-4.

MacLeod discusses Findley's career and describes his recently published novel, *Not Wanted on the Voyage*. It "is a tale of how the world could end . . . as fresh and meaningful today as when it was first set down in words." Findley is concerned with the environment, the position of women, and the threat of nuclear holocaust. He has little faith in the political structure to solve problems. Individuals, especially writers who can articulate what they see, must speak out.

C113 "71 Named to Canada's Top Honor." *The Toronto Star*, 28 Dec. 1985, pp. A1, A4.

In this announcement of Canadians appointed to the Order of Canada, Findley is listed as an Officer of the Order.

C114 Brydon, Diana. " 'It Could Not Be Told': Making Meaning in Timothy Findley's *The Wars*." *The Journal of Commonwealth Literature* [London], 21, No. 2 (1986), 62-79.

The Wars is concerned with how we make meaning through the shaping conventions of language and visual perception, experiences that those conventions seem incapable of controlling. Brydon discusses the interaction between text and narration in an effort to understand the method of *The Wars*. She focuses on the novel's obsession with what "could not be told," the limitations of language, and its turning to visual images to "circumvent, or at least complement, the limitations of telling." The text is organized around two spatial images: concentric circles "eddying around Robert's obscurely motivated saving of the horses," and an archaeological site where the researcher attempts to unearth fragments of the past and make it live again. *The Wars* develops a fictional language of images, patterns of repetition, and substitution to tell "what could not be told." Brydon discusses the use of animal images and citations of other texts which reinforce the novel's concerns with language and visual perception.

C115 Duffy, Dennis. *Sounding the Iceberg: An Essay on Canadian Historical Novels*. Toronto: ECW, 1986, pp. ii, iii, iv, 54, 64-66, 71.

Duffy's study of Canadian historical novels traces the genre's development "to its position among the serious fiction of our time." *The Wars* is one of four novels that marked the rebirth of the historical novel in the 1970s. Although Findley uses World War I as his setting, the novel is really about the imaginative reconstruction of the past. In the style of postmodern metafiction, the story-telling conventions are being examined. Findley also "plays with the conventions of fiction writing and history," and shows that history "can be shaped by the craftsman's hand." *The Wars* is unique in Canadian historical fiction in that it has nothing to do with a national vision of the war.

C116 "Findley, Timothy Irving Frederick." *International Authors and Writers Who's Who.* Ed. Ernest Kay. 10th ed. Cambridge: International Biographical Centre, 1986.

The entry lists publications, awards, appointments, and memberships.

C117 Fraser, John. "Timothy Findley." In his *Telling Tales.* Toronto: Collins, 1986, pp. 84–89.

In this essay on critics and sensitivity to criticism, Fraser relates how his negative review of *Can You See Me Yet?* (D146) affected Findley, how Margaret Laurence defended the play (C15), and how these affected Fraser.

C118 Hulcoop, John F. "Timothy Findley." *Dictionary of Literary Biography.* Vol. 53: *Canadian Writers Since 1960.* Ed. W.H. New. Detroit: Gale, 1986, 181–91.

Hulcoop profiles Findley and analyses his novels, plays, short stories, and radio and television work. He discusses recurring themes and images in Findley's work, autobiographical elements, and his portrayal of women. Findley was virtually unknown until Penguin published a paperback edition of *The Wars* in 1978. *Can You See Me Yet?*, "the most disturbing, moving, and revealing of all his fictions," is rarely performed. Hulcoop calls *The Wars* "a major achievement"; it "stands head and shoulders above the majority of Canadian novels . . . ." Hulcoop includes a brief bibliography of Findley's work, interviews with him, and critical articles, as well as a page from a work-in-progress (*The Telling of Lies*).

C119 Knickers, Suzi [Darling, Michael]. "Suzi Knickers' Book Bits." In *The Bumper Book.* Ed. John Metcalf. Toronto: ECW, 1986, pp. 116, 117.

This tongue-in-cheek literary gossip column relates that Ted Fields (*Revenge of the Nerds*) is planning to film *Famous Last Words*. Projected title: *Famous Last Nerds*. Another item reports that Findley is in South Korea for Timothy Findley Week.

C120   MacLeod, Jack. "The Importance of Not Being Earnest: Some Mutterings on Canadian Humour." In *The Bumper Book*. Ed. John Metcalf. Toronto: ECW, 1986, p. 83.
"Canadian book reviewers taken as a lump, should be taken as a lump." MacLeod relates how humourist Donald Jack dismissed *The Wars* in one paragraph as "an unacceptable distortion" of World War I (D23).

C121   Mathews, Lawrence. "Hacking at the Parsnips: *The Mountain and the Valley* and the Critics." In *The Bumper Book*. Ed. John Metcalf. Toronto: ECW, 1986, p. 199.
In this article on Canadian literary criticism, Mathews writes that an expert on the work of Frederick Philip Grove is said to have recommended to a friend not to read anything by Grove, but to read Findley instead.

C122   Sutherland, Fraser. "Frisking Laura Secord." In *The Bumper Book*. Ed. John Metcalf. Toronto: ECW, 1986, pp. 22, 23-24.
Sutherland relates how his review of *The New Canadian Poets: 1970-1975* in *The Globe and Mail* elicited a letter to the editor from Findley (B46). Sutherland complained that Canada's young poets were not rebelling against the older generation of poets and editors. Findley responded that they are engaged in "civil wars of a different and more mature kind . . . with their society, culture and governments." Sutherland suggests that Findley and others confuse aesthetics and ethics when they demand that artistic works be progressive and improving.

C123   Weiss, Allan. "Professing Support: In Defence of Academia's Role in Canadian Literature." In *The Bumper Book*. Ed. John Metcalf. Toronto: ECW, 1986, p. 138.
Weiss mentions Findley as one of the "central-Canadian realists" who was criticized by George McWhirter in a letter to *The Globe and Mail* (C110).

C124 Halpenny, Francess G. "The Worth of Imagination." *The Graduate* [Univ. of Toronto], March–April 1986, p. 21.

In her convocation address, Halpenny stresses the need for demonstrations of the worth of the mind and the imagination, especially in the field of the humanities. *Not Wanted on the Voyage* is such a demonstration. It picks up our literary and religious inheritance making "a new and different whole . . . which is eloquent and anguished about and to our own self-destructing world."

C125 Adachi, Ken. "Death of Duchess Frees Findley Novel." *The Toronto Star*, 28 April 1986, p. D1.

Famous Last Words could not be published in Britain until the death of the Duchess of Windsor because of the possibility of a libel suit. Although the book was cleared by lawyers for publication in Canada, Clarke, Irwin took out substantial libel insurance (see C54). Findley's "imaginative depiction of the duchess was so compelling it [was] hard not to believe that that was the way it really was." Adachi also mentions that a revised edition of *The Butterfly Plague* is being published. Findley says he is revising it because it is an "undisciplined piece of writing."

C126 McKenzie, M.L. "Memories of the Great War: Graves, Sassoon, and Findley." *University of Toronto Quarterly*, 55 (Summer 1986), 395-411.

The Wars shares with war literature of this century the common features of stark realism in the depiction of the horrors of war, an emphasis on war's psychological effect on the individual, and an ironic probing of the motivation and conduct of the war's leaders. McKenzie notes that "interesting and rewarding parallels" can be found in *The Wars* and the works of British soldier-writers like Robert Graves and Siegfried Sassoon, alluded to in Findley's novel. McKenzie discusses two series of comparisons between Findley's novel and the earlier works: "the presentation of psychological reactions to the war that stress its destructiveness" and the use of "motifs that offer cautious hope for mankind." In *The Wars*, examples of the psychological reaction McKenzie describes include irrational and sexual violence and reckless daring. Motifs that suggest hope include spiritualism, sympathy with animals, and the possibility of protest by an individual. Robert Ross's act of defiance was not political like Sassoon's, but was "a spontaneous response to his sudden recognition of the insanity of destruction."

C127 Hatch, Ronald. "Narrative Development in the Canadian Historical Novel." *Canadian Literature*, No. 110 (Fall 1986), pp. 92-94.

In this essay tracing the development of narrative technique in Canadian historical novels, Hatch writes that *The Wars* forces us not simply to observe history, but to confront it. The reader comes to realize that history does not exist as something given, but is continually reshaped by the present. Findley's narrative mode "allows him to develop a sense of history unfolding in time and still show that an individual can refuse to follow the 'forces of history' through the power of his moral judgement." His use of a researcher who combines scraps of historical information emphasizes the role of storytelling in the creation of history. The text not only conveys information about people in the past, it unites us with them. This has the effect of "calling the reader to the same kind of involvement in his own time."

C128 Slopen, Beverley. "Robertson Davies Tipped to Capture Coveted Fiction Prize." *The Toronto Star*, 21 Sept. 1986, "Book World," p. G10.

Slopen names *Not Wanted on the Voyage* as one of three Canadian novels short-listed for the Booker Award. She also mentions that Findley attended the launch party for Pierre Berton's book, *Vimy*. Findley loaned Berton his uncle's letters written during World War I which Findley used when writing *The Wars*.

C129 Slopen, Beverley. "How Findley Overcame Fear of Flying." *The Toronto Star*, 28 Sept. 1986, "Book World," p. G11.

Slopen describes how Findley overcame his fear of flying in order to accept a lucrative engagement in British Columbia. The promotional tour for *The Telling of Lies* is "probably the most extensive promotion tour a Canadian novelist has undertaken." Slopen describes the novel and the woman upon whom the character of Vanessa is based.

C130 Yanofsky, Joel. "Image of Body Out in Open on Beach in Maine Sparked Story." *The Gazette* [Montreal], 25 Oct. 1986, p. B8.

This article accompanies Yanofsky's review of *The Telling of Lies* (D124). Findley considers the novel a "political book," an exploration of the "ambiguous" and "deplorable" relationship between Canada and the United States. He describes the problems he encountered writing in the first person, feeling confined by the demands of the plot, and having to lead the reader through the narrative without giving away the ending. Mystery writer Georges Simenon was Findley's model for what he calls a "howdunit," rather than a "whodunit."

C131 Bale, Doug. "*The Telling of Lies* a Ground Breaker for Timothy Findley." *The London Free Press*, 5 Nov. 1986, p. C4.
Bale profiles Findley and discusses some of his political views. *The Telling of Lies* is a "ground breaker" for Findley in more than one respect. It is, for example, the first time he has written entirely in the first person. While the novel is "humorous, charming, engrossing, suspenseful," Findley is "dead serious" in his message that "we mustn't let politicians get away with things." Findley was inspired to write the novel by revelations of long-secret brainwashing experiments carried out in a Montreal hospital for the CIA. Findley's involvement with P.E.N. International reflects the concerns he expresses in *The Telling of Lies*.

C132 "Paperback Association Honors Findley Novel." *The Toronto Star*, 11 Nov. 1986, p. F2.
Not Wanted on the Voyage is one of two books named as Canada's outstanding paperbacks for 1986 by the Periodical Distributors of Canada.

C133 Everett-Green, Robert. "Summers of Sand and Shonagon Lend Color to Findley's Lies." *The Globe and Mail* [Toronto], 15 Nov. 1986, p. C1.
Everett-Green describes the Atlantic House Hotel and the summers that Findley spent there — background material for *The Telling of Lies*. Findley reminisces about some of the eccentric guests at the hotel and the "vanished society" they represent. He laments the hotel's demolition as well as the destruction of the nearby salt marshes.

C134 McGoogan, Kenneth. "Author's Gripping Tale Began as a Joke." *Calgary Herald*, 17 Nov. 1986, p. C1.
McGoogan writes that *The Telling of Lies* "began as a joke, developed in mysterious ways — and eventually turned into an iceberg." The novel was conceived on a beach in Maine when Findley visualized a series of scenes that ended with a dead body left on the beach. He joked with friends about the mystery novel he would write. The iceberg was "a complete surprise," but Findley followed his impulse and left it in. It is

the classic symbol of a lie and its resemblance to the U.S. Capitol Building has symbolic significance as well. Findley says this is his "most nationalistic novel."

C135 Woodcock, George. "Timothy Findley's Gnostic Parable." *Canadian Literature*, No. III (Winter 1986), pp. 232-37.

Findley is not the first Canadian writer to use the myth of the ark. Like his other novels, *Not Wanted on the Voyage* is a fiction on several levels and is best described as a "combination of fable and prose mock epic." While it is a book to be read "with the preoccupations of our own world in mind," it also draws on the traditions of primitive mythology, European fable, and classic children's animal stories. Woodcock finds that this novel gives "fictional expression to a view of the natural order and the nature of God" developed by the Gnostics. Findley's Yahweh is the Gnostic Demiurge "who has made the earth the place of death and cruelty that it is," and Lucy is the "messenger of light" who shares human fate.

C136 Benson, Eugene, and L.W. Conolly. *English-Canadian Theatre*. Toronto: Oxford Univ. Press, 1987, p. 60.

In the section on Radio Drama, Benson and Conolly describe how, between 1939 and 1965, the CBC became Canada's "National Repertory Theatre of the Air," employing 1,300 playwrights to write scripts for almost 8,000 dramatic broadcasts. The professionalism demanded by radio drama influenced the work of many dramatists who also wrote for the stage. Findley is mentioned as one of these.

C137 Booth, James, Susheila Nasta, Prabhu Guptara, John Thieme, and Charles Steele. "African, Caribbean, Indian, Australian, and Canadian Literature in English." In *The Year's Work in English Studies*. Ed. Laurel Brake. Vol. LXV. Atlantic Highlands, N.J.: Humanities, 1987, 733, 748.

In this annual review of critical work in English studies, the authors mention two articles about Findley: one by Coral Ann Howells comparing *The Wars* and Roger McDonald's *1915* (C87) and one by Linda Hutcheon on the narrative strategies of several Canadian writers (C73).

C138 "Findley, Timothy." *Who's Who in Canadian Literature 1978-88*. Ed. Gordon Ripley and Anne Mercer. Toronto: Reference, 1987.

The entry includes publications, awards, memberships, and biographical information.

C139 Miller, Mary Jane. *Turn Up the Contrast:* CBC *Television Drama Since 1952.* Vancouver: Univ. of British Columbia Press, 1987, pp. 3, 18, 190, 216, 228, 256, 267, 380, 383, 387.

Miller's study of CBC television drama is based on the premise that television drama is rarely taken seriously in Canada unless a programme like Findley's *The Paper People* hits "a nerve of controversy." Few collections of scripts exist, and those scripts that have survived are often "clean copies" that do not reflect on-set changes or post-production editing cuts. The televised ending of *The Paper People* is completely different from that of the script. Miller notes that television creates an outlet for Canadian writers like Findley who wrote for *The National Dream, The Whiteoaks of Jalna,* and *The Newcomers* series, and discusses the reasons the *Jalna* series was not the success it should have been. In the chapter on docudrama, Miller calls *The Paper People* a film in which "the values of documentary filmmaking are directly questioned using a purely 'fictional' film which is a highly personal statement by writer Timothy Findley and director David Gardner." *The National Dream,* an historical docudrama, was able to successfully "inscribe the landscape of our not-too-distant past on the imaginations of the audience." Miller suggests that the CBC commission more scripts from writers like Findley. Miller includes a Bibliography, Chronology of Series and Anthologies, Where to Find Material and a Cautionary Note, and A Checklist of Programmes.

C140 Moritz, Albert, and Theresa Moritz. *The Oxford Illustrated Literary Guide to Canada.* Toronto: Oxford Univ. Press, 1987, pp. 112, 123, 148, 170-71.

Findley is mentioned in the entry for Cannington, Ontario, where he has lived since 1964. The Kingston entry mentions his work as a disk jockey there in 1951-52, while the entry for Stratford lists him as an actor during the Festival's first season. Under Toronto, Findley's childhood homes, schools, and places of employment are described, as well as places in the city he has used as settings in his novels.

C141 Moss, John. "Timothy Findley." In his *A Reader's Guide to the Canadian Novel.* 2nd ed. Toronto: McClelland and Stewart, 1987, pp. 108-18.

Moss reviews Findley's major works in his book on the Canadian novel. The section on *The Wars* is a reprint, with slight revisions, from the 1981 edition of Moss's book (see D44). Moss finds many of the deaths in *Famous Last Words* gratuitous; "Findley seems fascinated by the narrative impact of death." The novel is "ambitious and curiously unsatisfying." It shows that "the greater truth is in effect the lie that can subsume even history — and give it back remade." *Not Wanted on the Voyage* is "a thing of wonder, one of the truly great books." Moss admires "the scope and diversity of his fiction . . . the power of his prose and the precision and clarity of his vision." Findley "invents with almost desperate abandon, discarding conventions of genre, defying the rules of history and chronology." *The Telling of Lies* is not really a mystery, it is "a puzzle." Moss finds the conclusion "contrived and portentous." The novel is worth reading because it is so well written and "because it consolidates major themes and motifs . . . relating to class, power, corruption, illusion, death."

C142 "PMC Awards." *Quill & Quire*, Jan. 1987, p. 20.
Not Wanted on the Voyage has been named one of the two outstanding English-language paperbacks of 1986 by the Periodical Marketers of Canada.

C143 Irwin, Joan. "A Wealth of Fine Films Lie Waiting in Canadian Novels." *The Toronto Star*, 17 Jan. 1987, "Air Waves," p. G7.
There are many Canadian novels and short stories which should be made into films. Some writers have had unhappy experiences when they worked on the film versions of their books. The collaboration of Findley and Robin Phillips on *The Wars* is an exception, "though the results of their labors would have to join the catalogue of distinguished duds." Findley is "one of the country's most imaginative and accomplished novelists." *Famous Last Words* and some of the short fiction in *Dinner Along the Amazon* would make good films.

C144 Mumford, Ted. "Findley Masters Mythic Distance." *Now* [Toronto], 29 Jan.–4 Feb. 1987, "Now Books," p. 33.
Mumford talks to Findley after his promotional tour for *The Telling of Lies*. They discuss that novel, what Findley is currently working on, and his acceptance of himself as a writer and as a person. Findley regrets the marketing strategy that labelled his novel a mystery. The question of "whodunit" is the least of mysteries; the greatest is "how people are

able to do such dreadful things to one another," sanctioned by society and government. Findley is working on a book of short stories and a "large" novel that deals "with here, now, and what I know of this moment in life in this place." It will be the first time he has written directly about homosexuality. He says he lived for a long time in the shadow of self-doubt, but he now concludes "that it's better for me to be me than anything else in the world."

C145 Adachi, Ken. "Findley Novel a Sell-Out in London Despite Critical Vitriol." *The Toronto Star*, 6 April 1987, p. B1.
Adachi writes that despite, or because of, negative reviews, Findley's "splendid" novel, *Famous Last Words*, is a sell-out in Britain. He quotes from several reviews, lamenting the British insularity that causes them to defend the Duchess of Windsor. Findley is quoted as being surprised that the British are so protective, since they had "lambasted" her when she was alive, and adds that none of the reviews really discuss the book as a work of fiction. He is "flabbergasted" that none of the critics picked up on his treatment of the Duchess as "a great iconic figure, an image of the time . . . ."

C146 "CBC to Dramatize Findley Novel." *The Globe and Mail* [Toronto], 10 April 1987, p. C9.
Famous Last Words will be dramatized on CBC Radio. Findley adapted his novel for the five-part series.

C147 Mietkiewicz, Henry. "Movie Makers Focusing on Canadian Authors." *The Toronto Star*, 28 July 1987, "In Print," p. C2.
Many Canadian books are being optioned for movie and broadcast rights. *The Telling of Lies* has been optioned to Nelvana Productions in Toronto, *Famous Last Words* to a U.S. company, and *Not Wanted on the Voyage* has been licensed to CBC Radio, with Findley doing the adaptation.

C148 Bolin, John S. "The Very Best of Company: Perceptions of a Canadian Attitude Toward War and Nationalism in Three Contemporary Plays." *American Review of Canadian Studies* [Washington, D.C.], XVII, No. 3 (Autumn 1987), 309-22.
Bolin analyzes three plays, including *Can You See Me Yet?*, which "display a remarkable thematic and stylistic unity which might be identified as typically Canadian." Bolin sees the thematic similarities as

66

the characters' prudence, their belief in the power of sacrifice, their distrust of persons and institutions of power, and their unique national identity. These themes are enhanced by the use of irony and presentational staging techniques. The real world/fictional world structure of *Can You See Me Yet?* "exhibits a special ability to use irony." Its documentary style permits the characters and the audience to move back and forth from the "real" asylum to the "fictional" past. Findley explores the theme of violence on a personal level as well as on a societal level. The theme of prudence is expressed through the entire cast's "determined life-wish" and the nature of sacrifice through Cassandra's desire to give her life for others. Findley is interested in "the theoretical underpinnings of identity: history and recognition."

C149 "Findley's 'Lies' Takes Top Paperback Fiction Prize." *The Vancouver Sun*, 18 Nov. 1987, p. D15.
The Telling of Lies has won first place in the paperback fiction category of the Authors Awards, co-sponsored by the Foundation for the Advancement of Canadian Letters and the Periodical Marketers of Canada. The judges called the novel "brilliantly written."

C150 Keith, W.J. "Apocalyptic Imaginations: Notes on Atwood's *The Handmaid's Tale* and Findley's *Not Wanted on the Voyage*." *Essays on Canadian Writing*, No. 35 (Winter 1987), pp. 123-34.
Keith discusses Margaret Atwood's *The Handmaid's Tale* and Findley's *Not Wanted on the Voyage* as two works that document the creation of worlds after a disaster or crisis. Both novels "provide intriguing evidence of the continuity within change that is so characteristic a feature of recent Canadian fiction." *Not Wanted on the Voyage* is "conspicuously post-modernist" and has connections with theories of deconstruction. Like Milton in *Paradise Lost*, Findley rewrites a biblical story for his own times, but as a postmodernist he can "weave anachronisms, absurdities, and parallels to the 1980s into the very fabric of his fictive vision." However, Findley follows Blake rather than Milton, writing within the tradition of Romantic revolutionary myth, where ". . . energy and justice wage war from below against the despotism of a sky-god." The novels share a concern with totalitarian politics and violence and have a feminist point of view. Read in the light of current controversy about critical theory and practice, they present a paradox. Both novels have an urgent message and rely on traditional

plot and characterization — elements that have no place in a post-modernist work. Keith speculates that this "Janus-like" quality is related to "the age-old Canadian reluctance to make a commitment to any extreme." He feels these novelists have been wise in refusing to embrace postmodernism wholeheartedly. The novels attest, in both form and content, "to a faith in human resilience against the dangerous rigidities of any excessively rationalistic system."

C151 Shields, E.F. "Mauberley's Lies: Fact and Fiction in Timothy Findley's *Famous Last Words.*" *Journal of Canadian Studies/Revue d'études canadiennes*, 22, No. 4 (Winter 1987-88), 44-59.
Traditionally, the reader learns passively from an historical novel, but Findley wants his readers to become involved, to question his version of history. To accomplish this he employs certain strategies, such as presenting "sensationalized, libelous portraits" of famous people who are still relevant to us. We might want to dismiss Findley's account as fabrication but he employs so much verifiable historical material that we cannot. The mysteries surrounding the murder of Harry Oakes, the flight of Rudolf Hess, and the plot to kidnap the Windsors "underline the difficulty of knowing what is the truth even when dealing with historical accounts." In *Famous Last Words*, Findley shows us that "although the difference between fact and fiction is often blurred, we must recognize that there is a difference and continue to attempt to discern one from the other."

C152 Bercuson, David J., and J.L. Granatstein. "Findley, Timothy." *The Collins Dictionary of Canadian History: 1867 to the Present.* Toronto: Collins, 1988.
The entry includes brief biographical information and notes Findley's "best known" works, *The Wars* and *Famous Last Words*.

C153 Gadpaille, Michelle. *The Canadian Short Story.* Perspectives on Canadian Culture. Toronto: Oxford Univ. Press, 1988, p. 110.
In this survey of the Canadian short story, Gadpaille briefly describes the stories collected in *Dinner Along the Amazon.* They are "gentle, leisurely tales" that recapture another era, "using a confiding first-person voice to document the pain of relationships between parent and child." Findley's characters are "the walking wounded in one sort of war or another."

C154 Hutcheon, Linda. *The Canadian Postmodern: A Study of Contemporary English-Canadian Fiction.* Toronto: Oxford Univ. Press, 1988, pp. 5, 6, 7, 10, 13-14, 17, 21, 28, 81, 118, 119, 132, 138, 139, 145, 161, 181, 190, 210, 212, 216-17.

This book is "an investigation not into the general phenomenon of postmodernism, but into the particular forms in which it appears in contemporary Canadian fiction." It consists of a series of essays on the subject, most of them previously published as journal articles, but "extensively rewritten" to fit the context of this study. Findley's work is discussed in several of the essays. In the Introduction, his novels are mentioned as examples of a postmodern challenge to the boundaries of "specifically 'high art genres,' " the deconstruction of British social and literary myths, a parody of biblical structures and narratives, "historiographic metafiction," and how novelists "use and abuse the conventions of the realist novel." *The Telling of Lies* is mentioned as a use and abuse of the traditional mystery novel form, and Findley's work is referred to several times as exemplifying various elements of Canadian postmodern fiction. See C73 and C92.

C155 Hutcheon, Linda. *A Poetics of Postmodernism: History, Theory, Fiction.* New York: Routledge, 1988, pp. ix, 5, 18, 84, 108, 114, 120, 145, 147, 149, 152-53, 155, 217.

The model that Hutcheon uses in this critical study of postmodernism is that of postmodern architecture; by analogy, she finds that "historiographic metafiction" characterizes postmodernism in fiction. Part I provides a framework in which to discuss postmodernism while Part II focuses on historiographic metafiction. Such works subvert realist narrative conventions, but through irony, not rejection. They are "both intensively self-reflexive and yet paradoxically also lay claim to historical events and personages." Findley's *Famous Last Words* is an example of this genre and Hutcheon discusses it throughout her book. Mauberley and the Duchess of Windsor illustrate the relationship between characters in novels and people in history. This novel, she concludes, "works to problematize the entire activity of reference." Hutcheon also mentions *The Wars* as an example of historiographic metafiction in which the readers see both the collecting of historical facts and the attempts to make narrative order of them.

C156 MacLulich, T.D. *Between Europe and America: The Canadian Tradition in Fiction*. Toronto: ECW, 1988, pp. 150, 225, 234, 237.

MacLulich finds an "identifiable tradition" of Canadian fiction which has been profoundly influenced by Canada's colonial origins and its existence in the shadow of its more populous and powerful neighbour, the United States. Canadian writing is poised between tradition and innovation, between old-fashioned certainties and "the disconcerting openness of postmodern art and philosophy." MacLulich cites Findley as one of the writers who reconsider their view of Europe as the repository of the best features of Western civilization. Findley examines humanity's destructive impulse in *The Wars* and explores the contradiction that exists in a culture that can produce both high art and excessive violence in *Famous Last Words*. Findley's work also represents a turning away from traditional modes of fiction toward various types of experimental writing.

C157 Murray, Don. "Seeing and Surviving in Timothy Findley's Short Stories." *Studies in Canadian Literature*, 13, No. 2 (1988), 200-22.

Murray's essay focuses on an important detail of Findley's characterization, "the act of looking at a person or thing." This act helps to define both individual characters and the relationships among characters, as well as telling us about the kind of world in which they operate. Findley's characters spend much of their time watching other people and themselves. They are "intense spectators, and the spectacle they behold is frequently unusual, if not bizarre." In the stories in *Dinner Along the Amazon*, optical imagery is Findley's primary means of "projecting his imagined world into the reader's purview." Murray describes Findley's visual images in the stories in the collection. In "Hello Cheeverland, Goodbye," the emphasis is on the "visual strangeness and the power of the eye to engage in combat." In "Lemonade" and "War," the child's problem centers on the actual mechanics of seeing and the difficulty of bringing the parent into focus. In "Losers, Finders, Strangers at the Door," visual images express a variation on Findley's self-reflection theme, while in "What Mrs. Felton Knew," they emphasize vision as communication. In "Dinner Along the Amazon," the optics focus on the breakdown of a relationship. Thus, in *Dinner Along the Amazon*, Findley "presents a variety of people communicating by visual means."

C158 "Timothy Findley." *Who's Who in the Writers' Union of Canada: A Directory of Members.* Toronto: Writers' Union of Canada, 1988.

The entry includes biographical data and information on publications, awards, and readings.

C159 Yanofsky, Joel. "Murder He Wrote: Timothy Findley Tackles a 'Howdunit' Novel." *Cross-Canada Writers' Magazine,* 10, No. 1 (1988), 5, 32.

Although each of his six novels has been a "departure and a challenge," Findley says he is not interested in fictional experiments. In writing *The Telling of Lies,* form followed content and what was a political novel, a study of the ambiguous relationship between Canada and the United States, evolved into a mystery. Findley rejects the mystery writer label and calls the novel more of a "howdunit" than a "whodunit." Writing this novel was "an unusually difficult experience." Findley found it challenging to lead the reader through the narrative without giving the plot away, to write in the first person, and to maintain a "balance of intelligence" between the narrator and the reader. Findley admires the mysteries of Georges Simenon.

C160 York, Lorraine M. *"The Other Side of Dailiness": Photography in the Works of Alice Munro, Timothy Findley, Michael Ondaatje, and Margaret Laurence.* Toronto: ECW, 1988, pp. 15, 16, 18, 19, 51-92, 93, 95, 96, 97, 98, 99, 100, 103, 104, 108, 114, 116, 119, 121, 122, 124, 126, 127, 134-35, 138-39, 147, 152, 153, 157, 165.

A revised and expanded version of York's Ph.D. dissertation, which examines the ways in which contemporary Canadian writers perceive the relationship between writing and photography (C176). Chapter ii is devoted to Findley's work.

C161 "CBC Turns Findley Novel into Five-Part Radio Series." *The Gazette* [Montreal], 5 Jan. 1988, p. C14.

This article calls *Famous Last Words* a "soaring drama" and describes the novel's plot and characters. Findley is quoted as saying that he "almost had to rewrite the book" to adapt it for radio. The author of the article found the scene between Edward VIII and Queen Mary "one of the most charming episodes" in the first broadcast of the series.

C162 Lacey, Liam. "Panoramic Findley Novel Makes Evocative Radio Drama." *The Globe and Mail* [Toronto], 8 Jan. 1988, p. D11.

The CBC Radio presentation of *Famous Last Words* is "a landmark of how well literature can be adapted to radio, and a tribute to both Findley's skill as a novelist and his unusually astute awareness of the demands of radio." The novel, with its "hopscotch" chronology and point of view, had to be extensively rewritten. The dramatization is "an addition to rather than a subtraction from the experience of reading the book."

C163 Crew, Robert. "Famous Last Words Makes Smooth Transition to Radio." *The Toronto Star*, 9 Jan. 1988, p. F3.

Crew reports that *Famous Last Words* has been "superbly adapted" by Findley for CBC Radio. Findley's acting experience was valuable in the process of turning the narrative of his novel into dramatic scripts. He had to nearly rewrite the book, juggling over thirty-five characters, writing new dialogue, dropping some of the prose, and making new bridges. Crew praises the cast of the five-part adaptation and feels that *Famous Last Words* "continues the proud tradition of thoughtful, accurately presented drama on CBC Radio."

C164 Salutin, Rick. "The Art of the Obituary. Or: If You're a Canadian Artist About to Die, It's Probably Better Not To." *This Magazine*, March–April 1988, pp. 38-40.

In this article about the obituary treatment of Canadian writers and artists, Salutin documents some recent "peccadilloes" that have appeared in print. *Maclean's* "managed not to blotch" the Margaret Laurence obituary (B53) by having Findley write it.

C165 Turner, Barbara E. "Doing the European Tour." *The Toronto Star*, 9 April 1988, "Saturday Magazine," pp. M1, M6.

Turner notes that books by Canadian writers have become popular all over Europe and describes the experiences of several Canadian writers on book promotion tours. Findley relates that on his recent tour of England negative reviews in the conservative press made *Famous Last Words* an overnight best-seller, but were "devastating personally."

C166 Kirchhoff, Jack. "From the Page to the Screen: Making the Most of Movies." *Quill & Quire*, May 1988, pp. 8-11.

In this article on making films based on Canadian novels, Kirchhoff mentions *Famous Last Words* and *The Telling of Lies* as titles optioned or sold to filmmakers by the Colbert Agency. Robertson Davies is quoted as saying that American-controlled distribution is what "killed" the film based on *The Wars*.

C167 Purdy, Al. "Death in the Family." *Saturday Night*, May 1988, pp. 85-86.
Purdy writes a tribute to poet Gwendolyn MacEwen and describes a memorial reading of her poetry at the St. Lawrence Centre in Toronto. Findley read, sounding "like the actor he once was."

C168 Slopen, Beverley. "Ottawa Professor Takes on a Venerable Paperback List." *The Sunday Star* [Toronto], 15 May 1988, "Book World," p. A19.
Findley has written the Afterword for Margaret Laurence's *The Diviners* (B57), one of the first titles in McClelland and Stewart's New Canadian Library series of paperback reprints. The success of the original series led to competitors, including Penguin who published several titles by Findley.

C169 Dunphy, Catherine. "Timothy Findley Loves the Slow Lane." *The Toronto Star*, 29 July 1988, "Life," pp. D1, D4.
Dunphy writes one in a series of articles about people who have chosen to live in small towns instead of urban centres. She talks to Findley and William Whitehead about their farm near Cannington, Ontario, the community there, and why they prefer living as they do. Findley calls the farm "an essential life-giving force in my life." The two writers relate the story of how they bought the farm and talk about their neighbours and their acceptance in the community. Findley says he feels they are responsible for passing the land on "in its good state."

C170 Boyce, Pleuke. "Canadian Writers Go Dutch." *Books in Canada*, Nov. 1988, p. 4.
In this article on the popularity of Canadian literature in Holland, Boyce mentions *The Wars* as one of a proliferation of Canadian works published there in 1979. Other Findley novels are available in Dutch bookstores, in both Dutch and English editions.

C171 Wilson, Peter. "Short Story Collection Gives Author Findley Hope for Genre's Future." *The Vancouver Sun*, 3 Nov. 1988, p. C5.

Originally *Stones* was to contain twelve stories, but Findley was unable to complete the last two when he temporarily gave up smoking. Another was rejected as being too similar to others in the collection. Findley is pleased that the short story is making a comeback in Canada and that John Fraser has re-established fiction in *Saturday Night*. Although his work is often referred to as "magic realism," Findley says he does not know what the term means. He begins a story by finding the voice, then the characters; ". . . literary fads don't even enter his mind." Findley was surprised when an editor pointed out that all the stories in *Stones* contain a reference to Toronto's Queen Street Mental Health Centre. "I knew that about a couple of the stories," he says, "but not that all of them had it in them. It was purely subconscious."

C172 Conn, Heather. "Echoes of Expo at Vancouver Festival." *Quill & Quire*, Dec. 1988, p. 18.

A staged dramatic reading of Findley's story "Stones" was performed by Findley and three actors at the Vancouver Writers Festival. It was "fondly received" at two sold-out performances.

Theses and Dissertations

C173 Yardley, M. Jeanne. "Fact, Fiction and Morality: A Study of Three Novels by Timothy Findley." M.A. Thesis Waterloo 1984.

Yardley examines Findley's use of historical material in his fiction, focusing on three novels. *The Wars* stresses individual experience in World War 1, "a disintegrating world where fascist values are attractive and accessible." In *The Butterfly Plague*, Findley considers North American as well as European society, and "issues a warning about the pervasiveness of the appeal of fascism." *Famous Last Words* extends this warning to artists as well as politicians by juxtaposing the historical and the fictional. Blending fact and fiction in these novels "serves to promote the reader's recognition of the writer's moral vision" and "aids in the presentation of his concern for the safety of twentieth-century society from the seductive appeal of fascism."

C174 Ingham, David Keith. "Mediation and the Indirect Metafiction of Randolph Stow, M.K. Joseph and Timothy Findley." Diss. British Columbia 1985.

Ingham discusses the range of "indirect metafiction" and the "spectrum of mediation" between reader, writer, and text. The analysis of three exemplary novels — Randolph Stow's *The Girl Green as Elderflower*, M.K. Joseph's *A Soldier's Tale*, and *Famous Last Words* — employs both postmodern and traditional critical approaches, "demonstrating them to be complementary." In chapter iv, "Timothy Findley and the Crystallization of Illusion," Ingham discusses how *Famous Last Words* demonstrates mediation by a writer whose text "crystallizes the illusions of fiction, then undercuts and exposes them."

C175 Novak, Dagmar. "The Canadian Novel and the Two World Wars: The English-Canadian Literary Sensibility." Diss. Toronto 1985.

The first Canadian novels about World War I were similar in their rhetorical and romantic tone and in their portrayal of war as a crusade. In the late 1920s a younger group of novelists shifted attention to the drudgery of war and to its violence. *The Wars* is a return to the romanticism of the early novels, while drawing as well on the characteristic motifs of the later ones — "gritty descriptions of the battle and the quest to give meaning to what is seen fundamentally as a dehumanizing ritual." The heroism of Findley's protagonist is not the same as the heroism of the early war novels but, for Findley, it is heroism nonetheless. In chapter iv, "Timothy Findley and the Return to the Great War," Novak focuses on *The Wars*.

C176 York, Lorraine Mary. " 'The Other Side of Dailiness': Photography in Recent Canadian Fiction." Diss. McMaster 1985.

York examines the ways in which four contemporary Canadian authors — Alice Munro, Michael Ondaatje, Margaret Laurence, and Timothy Findley — perceive the relationship between writing and photography. These writers have used photography in their fiction as both metaphor and structural motif. In chapter ii, " 'Violent Stillness': Timothy Findley's Use of Photography," York examines the relationships among photography, postmodernism, historical awareness, and memory. In his early works, Findley emphasized the "darker elements associated with the camera image: artificiality, lies, stifling fixity, and even fascism." In more recent works, he uses photography as an "invaluable preserver of the past." In the course of his career, Findley has broken down the barrier of photography as artificial object, letting it become a "metaphor for the processes of memory and writing . . . ."

York focuses her discussion on some of Findley's short fiction, *The Last of the Crazy People*, *The Butterfly Plague*, *The Wars*, and *Famous Last Words*. A published version of this dissertation is listed in C160.

Interviews

C177 Davis, Warren. Interview with Timothy Findley. *The Day It Is.* CBC TV, 27 Oct. 1967. (6 min.)

Davis interviews Timothy Findley and Richard Eastman, who recently returned from three years of theatre work with Alec Guinness in England, about their experiences there. Findley also talks about the fact that there is no longer a distinguishable Canadian actor type and why he left acting for writing. He says he realized that there was much he wanted to say that he could not express through acting. The end of the interview is garbled on the tape.

C178 Hutchinson, Helen. Interview with Timothy Findley. *Matinee.* Prod. Bill Castleman. CBC Radio, 1 Jan. 1969. (12 min.)

Hutchinson talks to Findley about the differences and similarities between acting and writing and about his writing methods. They also discuss what it means to be a Canadian writer and his reaction to Canadian critics.

C179 Gerussi, Bruno. Interview with Timothy Findley. *Gerussi!*. Prod. Diana Filer. CBC Radio, 18 Nov. 1969.

Gerussi interviews Findley about his career change from acting to writing and about the support he has received from Thorton Wilder, Ruth Gordon, and Garson Kanin. They also talk about *The Last of the Crazy People*, *The Butterfly Plague*, and his film, *Don't Let the Angels Fall*.

C180 Cameron, Donald. "Timothy Findley: Make Peace with Nature, Now." In his *Conversations with Canadian Novelists*. Toronto: Macmillan, 1973, pp. 49-63.

Cameron talks to Findley about his concern with man's relationship with nature and Findley reveals his motif: "Make peace with nature, now." He says that he loves many human beings but is "not particularly fond of the human race." Findley says that being a writer is "vicious." He describes the loneliness, the lack of security, and how his characters arrive on his doorstep, not leaving until he gets them down on paper.

His biggest problem as a writer is knowing how to select, afraid that he will not make himself clear. Findley also talks about his childhood, his acting career, and his desire to write plays. Cameron asks Findley why he likes cats and compares their "peaceful quality" and "incipient violence" to the atmosphere of his novels. Findley agrees, but says he wants them to be different. Cameron describes the novels as having to do with "the qualities of the mind which are private but give rise to public events and actions, the process by which fantasy becomes action." Findley calls this assessment "very apt." Cameron includes a brief biography and bibliography.

C181 Gibson, Graeme. "Timothy Findley." In his *Eleven Canadian Novelists*. Toronto: House of Anansi, 1973, pp. 115-49.

Gibson talks to Findley about his writing, particularly about his first two novels. Findley says he turned to novels because of the scope and freedom of expression they offer. He calls creative artists "very special people" because they have the gift of insight and "the ability to go from insight to paper." The greatest value writing has for him is that it allows his view of life to reach others. The Winslow family in *The Last of the Crazy People* represents a form of decadence, values, and attitudes no longer viable in contemporary society. Hooker's killing of his family was an act of love; it was also the only logical outcome of the story. Carson McCullers had an influence on this novel, which Findley calls "Southern Ontario Gothic." *The Butterfly Plague* gave Findley the chance to get involved in "larger ideas," and to explore the concept of perfection. He regrets not making some things more explicit in it but did not want to destroy the "dream-like, nightmare-like" character of the book. At this point in his career, Findley feels "confronted with a lot more of the closed doors that now I've got to get busy opening."

C182 Gibson, Graeme. Interview with Timothy Findley. *Anthology*. Prod. Alex Smith. CBC Radio, 31 March 1973. (25 min.)

Gibson interviews Findley about his work, as well as about the play and the novel as literary forms.

C183 Drainie, Bronwyn. Interview with Timothy Findley. "Artsworld." *Sunday Morning*. Prod. Richard Bronstein. CBC Radio, 21 May 1978. (11 min.)

Drainie discusses *The Wars* with Findley, as well as book censorship in Canada and the political situation in Quebec.

C184 Davidson, Joyce. "Timothy Findley." *Authors*. CBC-TV, 20 Oct. 1980. (30 min.)

Davidson describes Findley as "the gentle master of violence." They discuss the violence within him and the violence that emerges in his novels, as well as fire imagery in his work. Findley also talks about his "tumultuous" childhood, the personal attack he suffered over *The Last of the Crazy People*, his alcoholism, and his homosexuality.

C185 Aitken, Johan. "Long Live the Dead: An Interview with Timothy Findley." *Orbit* [Toronto], 11, No. 5 (Dec. 1980), 13-17. Rpt. (revised and expanded) in *Journal of Canadian Fiction*, No. 33 (1981-82), pp. 79-93.

This interview, as published in *Orbit*, focuses on *The Wars*. Aitken and Findley discuss the immediate and underlying causes of the novel's conception, the use of photographs, the characters of Barbara and Mrs. Ross, and the animal imagery. In commenting on the novel's point of view, Findley describes the shape of *The Wars* as an "avenue" that stretches back in time, lined with billboards upon which are selected photographs, "the images that I wanted to imprint of moments from that war, moments from Robert's life, moments from history . . . ." Additional material, including comments on the state of book production and marketing, literary criticism, and book reviewing in Canada, is included in the *Journal of Canadian Fiction* version of the interview.

C186 Summers, Alison. "An Interview with Timothy Findley." *The Malahat Review* [Univ. of Victoria], No. 58 (April 1981), pp. 105-10.

The themes and images in Findley's writing are the topics of this interview. Findley says his "most consistent" theme is that of "how people use other people; how we damage each other in our relationships." Writing that lasts has a political edge to it, but when writers introduce "party stuff," their work becomes boring. Findley describes war as what happens when ". . . people haven't bothered to pay attention in one way or another." A Hitler only articulates what many people want. He talks about the image of the garden in his work and how we must get back in touch with a childhood sense of our relationship with nature. Findley does not think he knows why there is so much fire imagery in his work but he says that ". . . it is so utterly destructive that to me it is the image of what is happening to us." When asked what he sees as "the enduring human values in the violent world" of his fiction, Findley suggests that it is the refusal to remain silent.

C187 Summers, Alison. "Interview with Timothy Findley." *Canadian Literature*, No. 91 (Winter 1981), pp. 49-55.

Summers focuses on Findley's acting career and his writing for the stage. Findley explains that he became an actor at the time of a resurgence of creative playwriting. He describes his involvement with the Stratford Festival, touring with *The Matchmaker*, and the influences of Ruth Gordon and Thorton Wilder. Wilder taught him that, if he had the "real gift" of writing, he had an obligation to do his best to use it. From his acting experience he gained a sense of rhythm and cadence, which has been valuable to writing fiction as well as plays. He says that even though he can reach more people through television, he prefers to write for live theatre, because it provides audience contact and "daring." Findley describes *John A. — Himself!* and the influence of Tennessee Williams on his dramatic work. He expresses regrets about giving up acting, but says, "I don't regret having made the choice to write at all."

C188 Meyer, Bruce, and Brian O'Riordan. "The Marvel of Reality: An Interview with Timothy Findley." *Waves*, 10, No. 4 (Spring 1982), 5-11. Rpt. (revised) in *In Their Words: Interviews with Fourteen Canadian Writers*. By Bruce Meyer and Brian O'Riordan. Toronto: House of Anansi, 1984, pp. 44-54.

Meyer and O'Riordan talk with Findley about *Famous Last Words*. In dealing with historical characters, Findley remarks that they should not be used "unless there's something that attracts you to them." He felt "timorous" approaching Ezra Pound's Mauberley as a character, but "had read enough to know that I was not misguided to be doing what I was doing." Mauberley is a hero because ". . . in writing what he does on the walls he must condemn himself and everything he stood for." Findley sees parallels between Mauberley's world and our own and agrees that Reaganism is the kind of nationalist sentimentality that contains the seeds of fascism. Mauberley and other characters in Findley's work are among the "best" people who "try to achieve the best that is in them." He remarks that what writers gain from other writers is "the strength to keep writing." In order to save our "dying civilization," Findley says we must pay attention to reality, both the squalor and the beauty.

C189 Hay, Elizabeth. "Summer Digest." *Sunday Morning*. CBC Radio, 1 Aug. 1982. (15 min.)

Taped in Toronto's Park Plaza Hotel before a dinner honouring him for *Famous Last Words*, Findley discusses that novel, his childhood, and his writing career. During the interview, he plays the piano, sings a childhood song, and reads from *Famous Last Words*. He says the novel explores the world of the 1930s and the nature of fascism. He has sympathy for Ezra Pound and the Duke and Duchess; sympathy is necessary in order to recognize the seeds of fascism in oneself. A fire destroyed his first book, written at 15 or 16. Findley says he does not know if that accounts for his frequent use of fire imagery and mentions fire scenes in the movies he saw as a child. Findley describes how Canadian publishers rejected his first two novels, and talks about the Canadian fear of success and his alcoholism.

C190 Hulcoop, John F. "A Frame of Fire." *Anthology*. Prod. Eithne Black. Exec. prod. Robert Weaver. Announcer Bronwyn Drainie. CBC Radio, 26 March 1983. (50 min.)

In this "impressionistic sketch of a multi-talented man," Hulcoop interviews Findley, discusses various aspects of his work, and Findley reads from several of his works. They talk about the effect of the world wars on children and on society. Characters like Iris in *The Last of the Crazy People* appear in many of his works. Findley says their close connection to reality makes it possible for them to survive. He comments that we must have "the courage to be oneself" and that fear is only a lack of love. All of his work explores fascism; madness is another important theme. Hulcoop sees Findley's vision of people's lives as a response to "the whispers of chaos" within ourselves.

C191 Finlay, Mary Lou. "Timothy Findley's War." *The Journal*. CBC-TV, 20 May 1983. (12 min.)

Finlay visits Findley at his farm where he is seen with some of his animals and singing at the piano. Findley discusses homosexuality, fascism, the role of the artist, and his inner violence. He is described by William Whitehead, editor John Pearce, and agents Stan and Nancy Colbert.

C192 Scott, Jay. "Dialogue on *The Wars*: A Symphony of Firsts." *The Globe and Mail* [Toronto], 10 Nov. 1983, p. E5.

Findley and director Robin Phillips discuss with Scott their collaboration on the film version of *The Wars*. Findley says Phillips taught him not to put too much down on paper since it hampers the actors. They both would have liked to have made *The Wars* as a television mini-series. Findley praises Phillips for his ability to transform material from one medium to another. They condemn the National Film Board's involvement in the film as "disgraceful" and lament the fact that Canadian artists have little opportunity to make films together. Findley and Phillips also talk about Glenn Gould's contribution to the film and American reaction to it.

C193 Goldie, Terry. "Interview." *Kunapipi* [Aarhus, Denmark], 6, No. 1 (1984), 56-67.

This interview took place in November 1982 at the McMaster University Fiction and Film Conference. Findley discusses several aspects of writing the screenplay for *The Wars* and working on its production. He calls Robin Phillips "a great director" who "is always open . . . to the creative inspiration of what might happen" and describes one such incident during the filming. Glenn Gould created the musical score using "found music" that was indigenous to the story's time and place. Findley also talks about *Famous Last Words*. He regrets that no one has written about the characters' iconic aspects — "a very important factor." Because he was working with historical figures, Findley says he had to be careful not to overstep "the boundaries of possibility" while still "heightening or underlining characters' traits." Findley, like some of his readers, finds the Quinn-Freyberg framing device problematic.

C194 Montador, Gordon. "Talking with Tiff." *The Body Politic* [Toronto], Oct. 1984, pp. 27-30.

Findley talks to Montador about growing up in a "lost" world of gentility and about his homosexuality. Findley says his family lived by a set of standards that no longer have meaning in modern society. He only gradually found a community where he felt accepted. Findley says that the stigma of homosexuality is still the same, "although the world you can move in is so much wider." However, he sees society entering a "very dark stage" where intellectuals, women, and homosexuals will be persecuted. William Whitehead joins the interview and they discuss his relationship with Findley, how he deals with Findley's fame, and with his drinking. Findley sees his drinking as an escape from "the real world" and, Whitehead adds, from being looked after. Findley says that life without Whitehead is "inconceivable." Although there have been homosexual characters in his novels, Findley has not written "a homosexual novel." He says he is working on one.

C195 Hough, Michael. "Timothy Findley: An Interview." *Public Works* [Univ. of Western Ontario], Spring 1985, pp. 55-59.
Findley discusses the episodic nature of his novels and writing process, describes how a writer stakes out "exploration rights" in the common body of material, and expresses his concern with fascism. The theme of fascism is present even in *The Last of the Crazy People*, which is about "the fascist regime" in a family. He also comments on writing about historical figures and describes how a Phyllis Webb poem redirected the writing of *Not Wanted on the Voyage*.

C196 Gzowski, Peter. Interview with Timothy Findley, Roger Lemelin, and Brian Moore. *Morningside*. CBC Radio, 14 Aug. 1985. (23 min.)
Gzowski interviews Timothy Findley, Roger Lemelin, and Brian Moore about their experiences writing for film. Findley says that adapting *The Wars* was "a happy experience," but adapting *The Last of the Crazy People* was a very unhappy one. He says the director has to love the book as well as being able to abstract from it an added dimension. They did not set out to make a commercial success of *The Wars*. A limited budget is responsible for its shortcomings. For Findley the writing process involves "watching and listening simultaneously" to let the story unfold cinematically. Instead of writing in chapters, he makes "jump-cuts" from scene to scene.

C197 Manguel, Alberto. "Timothy Findley: An Interview." *Descant* [The Detection Issue: The Culture of Crime], 16, No. 4—17, No. 1 [Nos. 51-52] (Winter 1985-86), 229-38.
Manguel interviews Findley about the detective novel he is writing, later published as *The Telling of Lies*. They discuss several aspects of detective fiction and Findley's work-in-progress, including Findley's favourite mystery writers, the real hotel and guests he is using in the work, how he first conceived the story "filmically," his difficulties plotting the novel, the use of coincidence, and some of the problems inherent in the genre. Findley says the work is "first and foremost a novel." He does not feel hampered by the detective form, but thinks that "form dictates wonderful things."

C198 Gabriel, Barbara. "Masks and Icons: An Interview with Timothy Findley." *The Canadian Forum*, Feb. 1986, pp. 31-36.

Gabriel talks to Findley about "the vision that informs his fiction." Much of the discussion focuses on *Not Wanted on the Voyage*, including the "formal problems of anthropomorphizing animals," the influence of Phyllis Webb's poem, the novel as a "critique of patriarchy," rereading Milton, and homosexual art. Findley says he relates his early female characters to his childhood experiences and speaks of the effect of his father's absence during World War II. They also discuss fascism, contemporary politics, and Canadian "snobbism."

C199 Sandor, Suzanne. "The Mystery of Violence." *Maclean's*, 27 Oct. 1986, pp. 10-12.

In this interview, Findley discusses his recently published novel, *The Telling of Lies*. He relates how it first came to him as a film image and comments on his use of the mystery genre. Findley tried to write the novel in the third person, but it did not give a sense of Vanessa "closing in" on the mystery. He stresses that he is not justifying murder, but exploring why other people do. He is not intrigued by violence, it is just that "I see it everywhere." Findley mentions the influence of gardens and of a book by a Japanese poet on this novel. Findley explains the work of P.E.N. International, and his involvement with it, and talks about his next writing projects.

C200 Gzowski, Peter. Interview with Timothy Findley. *Morningside*. CBC Radio, 30 Oct. 1986. (20 min.)

Gzowski talks to Findley about his new novel, *The Telling of Lies*. Findley describes the real hotel and the guest upon whom he based Vanessa. He also discusses the book's prison theme, the question of personal involvement, and writing in the first person as an old woman. Gzowski comments that he cannot see any difference between the American and Canadian characters. "That's partly the point," Findley replies. Findley reads the description of Nigel Forestead from the novel. The iceberg, he says, "provided a lot of fun" as well as the obvious symbolism. *The Telling of Lies* is about "the dark time"; to tell about that is his job as a writer.

C201 Crombie, Kevin. "Telling Truths. Kevin Crombie Talks with Timothy Findley." *RITES* [Toronto], Dec.–Jan. 1986-87, p. 9.

Although he does not think of himself as a "gay writer," Findley recognizes that ". . . there is . . . an awareness that is provided and fed by the fact of my homosexuality and what that has meant in the living of my life." Crombie reports that Findley's next novel will feature a gay character. Findley describes how he first met William Whitehead. He calls their relationship "the single most stabilizing aspect of his life." Findley talks about the theme of fascism in his work, contemporary politics, and his involvement with P.E.N. International. Crombie suggests that Findley's experiences and his understanding of them give his work an "undefinable gay sensibility."

C202   Twigg, Alan. *Strong Voices: Conversations with Fifty Canadian Authors*. Madeira Park, B.C.: Harbour, 1988, pp. 83-89.

This interview, which was done in 1984, focuses on Findley's writing techniques, themes, and "compulsions." Findley agrees that he is an explorer and not an explainer in his writing and that art should not be didactic. He trusts the "inner thing," what he calls "being obedient to the instinct to go and open that door." Findley feels that a large part of personal fear and violence comes from sexual tensions — the "walls" between men and women; ". . . all the walls have got to go" so people recognize their common humanity. Findley also talks about the violence in his writing and in himself, and about ignorance and culpability in the face of events like the Holocaust. He says he does not want to be like one of his characters who does something "Quixotic, saint-like and awful" to alert us about the dangers of authority and denying our instincts. Few people have recognized, he says, that the landscape of *Not Wanted on the Voyage* is that of Southern Ontario. Noah's ark is the blue barn on his farm.

C203   Buitenhuis, Peter. "The Return of the Crazy People." *Books in Canada*, Dec. 1988, pp. 17-20.

Buitenhuis talked to Findley in Vancouver where he read at the Writers Festival. They discuss connections between acting and writing, how Findley began writing, and the writers who have influenced him. Findley sees his acting as an "almost perfect apprenticeship." He began to write when he discovered his own story-telling voice and agrees that his work investigates a central figure that appears over and over again. Thorton Wilder, John Cheever, Joseph Conrad, T.S. Eliot, and W.H. Auden have been influential writers for Findley. He says that the sense of rhythm he got from acting is important to his work. "That's the thing that causes most of the rewrites, getting the rhythms right." He plans to write more in a dramatic form in the future, but says, "I'm not happy with myself as a playwright yet." Buitenhuis asks about Findley's subjects — "crazy people," war, and homosexuality. Findley admits to a "fascination with the world of the mentally excessive and unbalanced." It tells him about the human mind and spirit and the quest for perfection. The title story in *Stones* arose out of the experience of going to Dieppe to write a documentary. It is about "having to live the rest of your life in horror at having failed in everybody's eyes, but failed at something impossible." The Bragg and Minna stories are the first time that Findley has written directly about homosexuality. Findley says he did not consciously write a "gay" novel because he is opposed to "the ghettoizing of homosexuals. 'Gay' is a word I loathe and detest." These stories are also an exploration of his relationship with Marian Engel, and he plans to continue the series. Findley says he enjoyed writing the stories in *Stones*; it was a "new kind of writing, a new way of organizing a book."

Poems Dedicated to Timothy Findley

C204 Webb, Phyllis. "I Daniel." *The Literary Half-Yearly* [Univ. of Mysore, India] [A Canadian Issue], 24, No. 2 (July 1983), 95-99. Rpt. (revised) in *Poetry Canada Review*, 5, No. 2 (Winter 1983-84), 11. Rpt. (revised) in *Selected Poems: The Vision Tree*. Ed. Sharon Thesen. Vancouver: Talonbooks, 1982, pp. 151-54.

C205 Smithyman, Kendrick. "Screen Plays 1/2/3 — For Timothy Findley and William Whitehead." *Landfall: A New Zealand Quarterly* [Christchurch], 40, No. 3 (Sept. 1986), 277-80.

Awards and Honours

C206 Canada Council Junior Arts Award (1968).

C207 Armstrong Radio Drama Award for *The Journey* (1971).

C208 _____ , and William Whitehead. ACTRA Best Documentary Writer Award for *The National Dream* (1975).

C209 City of Toronto Book Award for *The Wars* (1977).

C210 Governor General's Award for *The Wars* (1977).

C211 Chairman, Writers' Union of Canada (1977-78).

C212 Ontario Arts Council Award (1977-78).

C213 Author of the Year, Periodical Distributors of Canada (1978).

C214 Canada Council Senior Arts Award (1978).

C215 _____ , and William Whitehead. ANIK Best Documentary Award for *Dieppe, 1942* (1979).

C216 Honorary D.Litt., Trent Univ. (1982).

C217 Author of the Year, Periodical Distributors of Canada (1983).

C218 Canada Council Senior Arts Award (1983).

C219 Author of the Year, Canadian Booksellers' Association (1984).

C220 Author of the Year, Periodical Distributors of Canada (1984).

C221 Honorary D.Litt., Univ. of Guelph (1984).

C222 Canadian Authors Association Literary Award for *Not Wanted on the Voyage* (1985).

C223 CNIB Talking Book of the Year Award for *Not Wanted on the Voyage* (1986).

C224 Officer of the Order of Canada (1986).

C225 Periodical Marketers of Canada Award for *Not Wanted on the Voyage* (1986).

C226 President, P.E.N. International Association of Writers in Canada (1986).

C227 Foundation for the Advancement of Canadian Letters and Periodical Marketers of Canada Annual Award for *The Telling of Lies* (1987).

D Selected Reviews (Books, Plays, Television, and Films)

Selected Book Reviews

THE LAST OF THE CRAZY PEOPLE

D1 Grosskurth, Phyllis. "New Canadian Novels." Rev. of *The Last of the Crazy People*, by Timothy Findley; *Mirror on the Floor*, by George Bowering; and *Willows Revisited*, by Paul Hiebert. *Saturday Night*, May 1967, pp. 39, 41.

Grosskurth compares *The Last of the Crazy People* and George Bowering's *Mirror on the Floor*, which are both about the devastation of a child's psyche caused by the private anguish of adults. The opening of Findley's novel is "tentative" and "derivative of countless other undistinguished openings." The novel's greatest strength is Findley's "evocation of Hooker's bewildered sense of a bewildering world," but the "brooding shadow of Faulkner hangs so ponderously over *The Last of the Crazy People* that any real originality is obscured."

D2 Clute, John. "Mom's Mad, Dad's Repressed, Sonny's Silly." *The Globe Magazine* [*The Globe and Mail*] [Toronto], 3 June 1967, p. 27.

The Last of the Crazy People, like early Truman Capote, is "moody, subtropical and terribly airless." Despite the fact that Southern Gothic was worn out years ago and Findley places his version of it in Toronto, he almost makes it work. Findley presents his characters without digression, letting them reveal themselves through dialogue. He handles the "milieu he lifted from Capote . . . with verve and a compelling terseness, without losing any of the humidity, moodiness or compulsiveness . . . ."

D3 "Books in Brief." Rev. of *The Last of the Crazy People*, by Timothy Findley; *Epitaphs of Our Times: The Letters of Edward Dahlberg*, by Edward Dahlberg; and *Manhattan Project: The Untold Story of the Making of the Atomic Bomb*, by Stephane Groueff. *The Telegram* [Toronto], 24 June 1967, "The Telegram Showcase," p. 22.

Findley's "clean, concise, prose in the gradual build-up toward a terrifying climax makes this one of the best Canadian works to come out this season."

D4 Boucher, Anthony. "Criminals at Large." *The New York Times Book Review*, 16 July 1967, p. 14. Rpt. in *Contemporary Literary Criticism: Excerpts from Criticism of the Works of Today's Novelists, Poets, Playwrights, Short Story Writers, Filmmakers, and Other Creative Writers*. Ed. Jean C. Stine. Vol. xxvii. Detroit: Gale, 1984, 140.

The Last of the Crazy People is "almost as pleasing as its odd title." Its "surprisingly gentle, nostalgic quality . . . is wholly charming," though it may seem at odds with the tragic story.

D5 Fulford, Robert. "Deep in the South (of Ontario)." *The Toronto Star*, 29 July 1967, p. 26.

Findley follows the Southern novel conventions almost to the last detail and is "just a little self-conscious about this." He has narrative ability and his grasp of dialogue is excellent, but his approach is "almost totally humorless" and most of the book is "unrelieved gloom."

D6 Parton, Margaret. "A Sad Song of Eleven Summers." *Saturday Review* [New York], 5 Aug. 1967, pp. 36-37. Rpt. in *Contemporary Literary Criticism: Excerpts from Criticism of the Works of Today's Novelists, Poets, Playwrights, Short Story Writers, Filmmakers, and Other Creative Writers*. Ed. Jean C. Stine. Vol. xxvii. Detroit: Gale, 1984, 140-41.

Findley has an actor's ear for dialogue and an actor's eye for scenes, some of which will linger in the mind for a long time. *The Last of the Crazy People* is not light summer reading, but ". . . it says something important, and says it with both craftsmanship and compassion."

D7 Dault, Gary Michael. "Fiction Chronicle." *The Tamarack Review*, No. 45 (Autumn 1967), p. 120.

The Last of the Crazy People is "such a skillful delineation of a houseful of neurotics" that we are led to believe that Hooker's solution is the only one possible. While there is nothing new in the novel structurally or stylistically, Findley "tells his story well, with precision and with a quite nerve-wracking intensity."

D8 Rosengarten, H.J. "Innocence Confused." Rev. of *The Sparrow's Fall*, by Fred Bodsworth; *The Last of the Crazy People*, by Timothy Findley; and *Little Portia*, by Simon Gray. *Canadian Literature*, No. 36 (Spring 1968), pp. 78-79.

The chief strength of this novel lies in the author's ability to "describe the response of the naïve or untrained mind to new areas of experience." It captures the irrational logic of a child's mind without treating childhood sentimentally. It "only too obviously" echoes Southern Gothic style, but Rosengarten finds the climax "convincing and satisfying."

D9   Thompson, Kent. Rev. of *Aboveground*, by Jack Ludwig; *Knife on the Table*, by Jacques Godbout; and *The Last of the Crazy People*, by Timothy Findley. *The Fiddlehead* [Univ. of New Brunswick], No. 76 (Summer 1968), p. 91.

Thompson read *The Last of the Crazy People* after seeing the "excellence" of Findley's script for *The Paper People*. The central moral concern of both works is "love is dangerous because it leads to destruction." The novel invites comparison with F. Scott Fitzgerald, William Faulkner, and Flannery O'Connor, but Findley has "accepted their standards and lessons rather than their superficial characteristics," and thus his novel has the individuality of his own particular skill. It is "a most satisfying work of art."

D10   Bowering, George. Rev. of *The Last of the Crazy People*. *The Canadian Forum*, June 1968, p. 70.

As a reader, Bowering found *The Last of the Crazy People* "easy to read" but, as a critic, he did not enjoy it as much. We know the novel's characters from "Southern Gothic family horrors," and there is a "kind of accomplishment in telling a story based on a literary cliché well." He wonders whether Findley is "having us on . . . if he isn't, he could use a little irony."

D11   Stedmond, J.M. "Letters in Canada: 1967. Fiction." *University of Toronto Quarterly*, 37 (July 1968), 386.

The Last of the Crazy People is "an impressive first novel." The story is told with "crisp economy" and the characters are "firmly captured." The conclusion might be "less sensational," but Stedmond concludes that Findley is "a talent to keep an eye on."

D12   Hill, Douglas. "Unfolding Timothy Findley." *The Globe and Mail* [Toronto], 8 Oct. 1983, "Entertainment," p. 13.

Hill praises the novel's atmosphere and depth of setting. The characters are "realized economically, fleshed out with careful brushstrokes of

mannerism and speech." It is "an accomplished and powerful novel."
Hill includes Findley's comments on his difficulty getting the novel
published, the film version of *The Wars*, his advice to new writers, and
his current work-in-progress.

THE BUTTERFLY PLAGUE

D13 Tannenbaum, Earl. *The Library Journal* [New York], 15 April
1969, p. 1649.
"The reader who likes his symbolism writ large will enjoy this
brooding legend of a darkling time . . . ." Metaphors of good and evil,
hope and despair, death and rebirth are woven together "with bright
threads of expressionism and a lyric style."

D14 Engel, Marian. "The Year of the Novel Brings a Grab-Bag." Rev.
of *Bullet Park*, by John Cheever; *Mr. Bridge*, by Evan S. Connell; *Make
Yourself an Earthquake*, by Mark Dintenfass; *The Butterfly Plague*, by
Timothy Findley; and *Terra Amata*, by J.M.G. LeClezio. *The Toronto
Star*, 19 April 1969, p. 30.
Engel suggests that Findley's use of fantasy and his "conversational
manner" are well-suited to a novel located in Hollywood in the 1930s.
Findley "sidles up" to his material, dealing with blood-lust, Nazism,
family feelings, and haemophilia "with delicacy and humor." Engel
wonders why several Canadian novelists are writing about Hollywood.

D15 Engel, Marian. Rev. of *The Butterfly Plague*. *The Telegram*
[Toronto], 13 May 1969, Sec. 3, p. 5.
Engel criticizes *The Butterfly Plague* for characters who "are un-
memorable and lacking in substance." The author's stated intent is to
relate the novel to theatre of the absurd, "but the book is fey and empty
at the core." Engel praises the good writing, especially the dialogue, and
Findley's ability to sustain the fantasy throughout the work. "Findley's
imagination is capable of lovely conceptions, but they do not make a
satisfying novel."

D16 "Uncomic Strip." *TLS: The Times Literary Supplement* [Lon-
don], 5 March 1970, p. 241. Rpt. in *Contemporary Literary Criticism:
Excerpts from Criticism of the Works of Today's Novelists, Poets,
Playwrights, Short Story Writers, Filmmakers, and Other Creative
Writers*. Ed. Jean C. Stine. Vol. xxvii. Detroit: Gale, 1984, 141.

This review compares *The Butterfly Plague* to a film, or rather to "an appreciative description of a fantastic film." But Findley as a novelist cannot rival a film director's pace, and the novel "proceeds more slowly than can have been intended." Its many atrocities seem to be presented for their "pictorial value rather than for any literary purpose." While there is occasionally "a flicker of Firbank in the writing . . . generally, the book is too stodgy, long-winded and mirthless to make the comparison worthwhile."

CAN YOU SEE ME YET?

D17 Lane, William. Rev. of *Can You See Me Yet?. Quill & Quire*, Nov. 1978, p. 30.
Can You See Me Yet? is a "difficult play" that reveals its meaning only on the second or third reading. Its difficulty results partly from the large number of characters, only a few of them clearly delineated and all of them constantly shifting roles. The play is "wonderfully atmospheric" and has a number of "shimmering monologues." It is evidence of the "new maturity of the Canadian theatre."

D18 McCaughna, David. Rev. of *Nothing to Lose*, by David Fennario; and *Can You See Me Yet?*, by Timothy Findley. *Quarry*, 28, No. 3 (Summer 1979), 85-86.
The National Arts Centre, "the most unnecessary, wasteful, and preposterous performing arts edifice in the country," is almost equally to blame for its sponsorship of *Can You See Me Yet?* as is the playwright for writing a play "that is top heavy with pretensions, creaking with inane symbolism, riddled with monotonous themes and dreary to the point of stultification."

D19 Wasserman, Jerry. "Integral/Fractional." Rev. of *Can You See Me Yet?*, by Timothy Findley; *The Dismissal*, by James Reaney; *Ploughmen of the Glacier Seven Hours to Sundown*, by George Ryga; and *The Hearing*, by David Lewis Stein. *Canadian Literature*, No. 85 (Summer 1980), p. 107.
The plays reviewed here share a concern with the "ideas of personal integrity and social reform." Wasserman finds echoes of Margaret Atwood, Margaret Laurence, Ingmar Bergman, and William Faulkner in Findley's "rich and sensitive play." The play's primary images are

"blatant," but not "glib," and Findley manages "beautifully done" transitions between Cassandra's family life and the asylum. His triumph is in maintaining a "hard edge . . . never allowing lapses into pathos or cliché."

THE WARS

D20   Lecker, Robert. Rev. of *The Wars. Quill & Quire*, Oct. 1977, p. 7.

The Wars, as a documentary novel, fails in its presentation of the documented material, "just as it fails to find a unifying metaphor." Findley asks us to accept the novel's discontinuous structure "as a form of truth," but fails to make the lack of structure meaningful. He comes closest to creating something of value in his "*Equus*-like" portrayal of Robert Ross.

D21   Martin, Peter. "An Alternate Selection." *The Canadian Reader*, Oct. 1977, pp. 6-7.

Martin praises *The Wars* as "one of the most powerful, best-crafted . . . stories it has ever been my uncomfortable pleasure to read." Findley writes about World War I as though he had been there. Martin predicts that *The Wars* will win the Governor General's Award.

D22   Scott, Chris. "Hello to All That." *Books in Canada*, Oct. 1977, pp. 8-9.

The "intercutting" between past and present in *The Wars* provides a "distancing counter on an otherwise well-nigh unmanageable subject." Findley's combat scenes equal anything by Robert Graves or Siegfried Sassoon. It is "an extraordinarily beautiful book . . . not just on the level of metafiction or popular history . . . but on the deeper archetypal level of myth . . . a rare achievement."

D23   Jack, Donald. "Two Views of War." Rev. of *A Terrible Beauty: The Art of Canada at War*, by Heather Robertson; and *The Wars*, by Timothy Findley. *The Globe and Mail* [Toronto], 15 Oct. 1977, p. 43.

The Wars, writes Jack, illustrates our "national character: a superficial sensitivity to others, a lack of interest in people." He regrets having to say that Findley's portrayal of the war is "an unacceptable distortion."

See C120.

D24 Powell, Marilyn. "Missing in Action." *Maclean's*, 17 Oct. 1977, p. 84.

"At its best, Findley's novel is a shattering, uncanny recapturing of the original decency and terror of the war poets," but his literary device — that we are researchers trying to piece together the past through letters and photographs — is "clichéd, bland and in the way."

D25 Hill, Douglas. "Powerful, Devastating Canadian War Novel Demands Superlatives." *The Toronto Star*, 22 Oct. 1977, p. D7.

The Wars is not just another novel about men in battle; it is about each character's private wars "against the pressures, intrusions and assaults that threaten survival." Findley's narrative device of having a researcher reconstruct Robert Ross's story is skillful and unobtrusive. The writing "operates at a level of emotional intensity and sheer voltage that allows no reader distancing." Hill calls Findley "a mature and controlled artist at the peak of his remarkable powers."

D26 Atwood, Margaret. "An Important Book, for Many Reasons." *The Financial Post* [Toronto], 12 Nov. 1977, p. 6. Rpt. (revised) in *Second Words: Selected Critical Prose*. By Margaret Atwood. Toronto: House of Anansi, 1982, pp. 290-95.

The Wars is an important book because it is an example of certain aspects of book publishing and reviewing in Canada. It is also important in its own right, an "accomplished novel" by a "totally serious writer." Findley's dramatic background shows in the "tightness, the drama and the visual quality" of his writing. Robert Ross is an essentially Canadian hero "vilified by the society that produced him," and *The Wars* is an example of Southern Ontario regional writing. Findley has a tendency to "creep along the edge of sentimentality when it comes to our furry and feathered friends." Atwood concludes that the "starkness and power of its story . . . justifies, for once, the hyperbole on the jacket."

D27 Saunders, Tom. "Slow Start Mars Good Novel of War." *Winnipeg Free Press*, 19 Nov. 1977, p. L6.

The Wars is "at best a good novel." The first 121 pages are "pedestrian and dull," although the pace does pick up. Robert Ross who is at first "a wooden character . . . develops into a much more interesting person" in the final scenes, the best part of the novel.

D28 Novak, Barbara. "Novel about Great War Captures Bewildered State of a World Gone Mad." *The London Free Press*, 26 Nov. 1977, p. B3.

The realities of World War I, as conveyed by *The Wars*, are a far cry from the idealistic and romantic dreams of glory with which Robert Ross grew up. Findley has captured the "frantic, bewildered state of a world gone mad." It is the sense of immediacy he creates that makes the novel so forceful. *The Wars* should be required reading in every high school history course.

D29 Bannon, Barbara A. Rev. of *The Wars*. *Publishers Weekly* [New York], 20 Feb. 1978, p. 105.

Findley's "poignant" novel reminds Bannon of Erich Maria Remarque's *All Quiet on the Western Front* and Ernest Hemingway's war novels. "Crystalline prose, free of excess, and characters suffused with an illuminating realism contribute to the stature of this important and searing novel."

D30 Galloway, Myron. "Findley's Wars." *The Montreal Star*, 6 May 1978, p. D3.

The Wars is not only Findley's best work, but "among the finest novels to be published in this country in the past couple of decades." The novel has many levels of meaning, and Findley writes with "enormous sensitivity." His imagery is "vividly poetic," and the novel is infused with compassion for all living things. *The Wars* has established Findley as one of Canada's most important literary artists.

D31 Taylor, Michael. Rev. of *The Wars*. *The Fiddlehead* [Univ. of New Brunswick], No. 118 (Summer 1978), pp. 172-74. Rpt. in *Contemporary Literary Criticism: Excerpts from Criticism of the Works of Today's Novelists, Poets, Playwrights, Short Story Writers, Filmmakers, and Other Creative Writers*. Ed. Jean C. Stine. Vol. xxvii. Detroit: Gale, 1984, 141-42.

Some subjects, Taylor observes, have a "built-in intransigence to literary treatment because their historical reality . . . surpasses anything that the creative imagination can make of them." It took considerable nerve to "write a novel squarely about the unspeakable reality of the 1914-18 war in order to make that reality even more unspeakably real." Findley camouflages the fiction by presenting the story as a type of historical document. This technique, however, often makes Robert

Ross's story seem "forced and untrue." The novel "demands our an-guished sympathy without really having done enough to earn it."

D32 Gibson, Kenneth. "Broken Light." *Ontario Report*, July 1978, p. 38.
In order to understand World War I, we set down what we can know, we "research the field." What Findley has done is to "leave the Researcher in the book" as a way of keeping the reader in two worlds, and "of seeing the work that went into the novel as part of its cumulative effect." Findley excels in depicting the "texture" of Robert Ross's life, but *The Wars* "isn't quite satisfying." Perhaps this is because the researcher also had to write the book, "as if the work had summoned up too much for the novelist to handle in full flexibility."

D33 Edwards, Thomas R. "The Grim War and the Great War." Rev. of *Better Times Than These*, by Winston Groom; and *The Wars*, by Timothy Findley. *The New York Times Book Review*, 9 July 1978, pp. 14, 26. Rpt. in *Contemporary Literary Criticism: Excerpts from Criticism of the Works of Today's Novelists, Poets, Playwrights, Short Story Writers, Filmmakers, and Other Creative Writers*. Ed. Jean C. Stine. Vol. XXVII. Detroit: Gale, 1984, 142.
The Wars is "elegantly written and structured and well aware of what can't be said about important human experiences." Robert Ross is an intriguing figure and Findley's fictional method of reconstructing his story "stresses the human strangeness that even war can't break down." We must "puzzle out" not only Ross, but many of the other characters. The novel has flaws — its poetic prose sometimes becomes overripe and its climatic moment is over-prepared for by "insistent" imagery of horses and fire — but it is an "impressively sustained meditation on how war crystallizes an unfinished personality even while destroying it."

D34 "Briefly Noted: Fiction." Rev. of *The Wars*. *The New Yorker*, 21 Aug. 1978, p. 94.
The familiar events depicted in *The Wars* "take on a midnight beauty, the ferocious truth of a work of art," in Findley's "firm hands, observant eyes, and knowing imagination."

D35 Thompson, Eric. "Of Wars & Men." Rev. of *The Wars*, by Timothy Findley; *Out of the Shadows: Canada in the Second World*

War, by W.A.B. Douglas and Brereton Greenhous; and *Blueprint*, by Philippe Van Rjndt. *Canadian Literature*, No. 78 (Autumn 1978), pp. 99-100.

Findley's characterization of Robert Ross is "sure-handed — realistic, never sentimental." Ross is a true hero and Findley has "achieved something very fine in his delineation of the human spirit." His narrative method and powers of description are effective, and his story is "carefully reconstructed," providing the reader with a "new sense of the reality of the past." The "honesty and intensity" of *The Wars* in expressing the horror of armed combat make this book "one of the most remarkable novels of war ever published."

D36 Buitenhuis, Peter. "Wars Unseen." *West Coast Review* [Simon Fraser Univ.], 13, No. 2 (Oct. 1978), 52-54.

Paul Fussell has described the persistent power of World War 1 over the modern imagination and how closely the battle images of that war correspond to Northrop Frye's version of the ironic mode in literature. When the world of experience corresponds to an established literary mode, ". . . it becomes doubly attractive to a writer." Findley's novel is an example of this phenomenon. Many of the novel's characters are "self-destructive," and war provides "the most plausible background and metaphor" for a story obsessed with death and its consequences. Buitenhuis criticizes the book's narrative methods, its "infelicities," and Findley's "easy way out" of the question of responsibility, but pronounces *The Wars* "a remarkable book."

D37 Stevens, Peter. "Warring Spirits." *The Ontario Review* [Princeton, N.J.], No. 9 (Fall–Winter 1978-79), pp. 107-08.

A "furious vision of man's destruction of his world and its creatures leads Findley into a style that emphasizes the grotesque terrors of both external action and interior griefs." The theme of brutalized love often dissipates the energy of Findley's vision of war. Stevens finds that the present world of the researcher has not been assimilated into the fictional world of the past and thus, intrudes on the realism of the novel. Nevertheless, the novel has "undeniable power in its presentation of Ross's involvement with war."

D38 Davenport, Gary T. "A Canadian Miscellany." Rev. of *Toronto Short Stories*, ed. Morris Wolfe and Douglas Daymond; *Night Flights: Stories New and Selected*, by Matt Cohen; and *The Wars*, by Timothy

Findley. *Sewanee Review* [Univ. of the South, Sewanee, Tenn.], 87, No. I (Winter 1979), xxi–xxii. Rpt. in *Contemporary Literary Criticism: Excerpts from Criticism of the Works of Today's Novelists, Poets, Playwrights, Short Story Writers, Filmmakers, and Other Creative Writers.* Ed. Jean C. Stine. Vol. xxvii. Detroit: Gale, 1984, 142.

Davenport finds much to praise in *The Wars*: the characters are convincing, the story is well-told, the scenes follow each other with "sure logic," and thematic interest arises naturally from the novel's events. But he complains of its "stylistic slickness," "telegraphic one-liners," "typographical cleverness," and "studied sensitivity" of the prose. Nevertheless, the book is a "substantial performance."

D39 Hanlon, Michael. "One of the Best Canadian Novels Printed." *Sunday Star* [Toronto], 7 Jan. 1979, p. B6.

The Wars is "one of the best Canadian novels ever to see print." It is "terribly, terribly brutal," "masterful," and Hanlon marvels that it was written in just three months.

D40 Taylor, Mark. "Bourne Again." Rev. of *The Middle Parts of Fortune*, by Frederic Manning; and *The Wars*, by Timothy Findley. *Commonweal* [New York], 19 Jan. 1979, p. 27.

In *The Wars*, Findley "gets it right"; he portrays what it was like to be there. His account of a chlorine gas attack is "as realistic, and as terrifying, and as moving" as a similar one in the poetry of Wilfred Owen. Findley's subject is not the War, but the wars — all the "monstrosities" his hero is caught up in. His theme is life, "its value, its would-be preserver, and its multiform enemies."

D41 Stuewe, Paul. "War Is Horrible but at Least It Doesn't Come Crawling Out of the Woodwork." Rev. of *The Wars*, by Timothy Findley; *Dual Allegiance*, by Ben Dunkelman; *Love in the Dog House*, by Molly Douglas; *Killing Time*, by Sandy Fawkes; and *Spiders*, by Richard Lewis. *Books in Canada*, Feb. 1979, p. 31.

A re-reading of *The Wars* in its just-published paperback edition affirms for Stuewe that the novel is "structured in a complex, interesting manner . . . and certainly reflects the author's absorption in his chosen historical milieu." But, as a novel of character and incident, it is not a success.

D42 Peterman, Michael. "English-Canadian Fiction in 1977." *Journal of Canadian Studies/Revue d'études canadiennes* [Trent Univ.], 14, No. 1 (Spring 1979), 94-96.

The Wars is "one of the most remarkable novels written by a Canadian." Findley uses war as a "particular environment in which life can be more clearly perceived." *The Wars* is a love story as well, but not in the conventional sense. The innocent love that Robert Ross shares with his sister "lies deep in the young man as soldier." The novel's circular structure and images approximate the narrator's search for the essence of Ross's life and draw the reader constantly inward toward his heroic act. In war, violence obscures a man's testament; in art, Findley shows, violence can be used to clarify it.

D43 Boyd, William. "War in Fiction." Rev. of *The Wars*, by Timothy Findley; *War and Remembrance*, by Herman Wouk; and *Going After Cacciato*, by Tim O'Brien. *London Magazine*, Nos. 5-6 (Aug.–Sept. 1979), pp. 125-26.

Writers of war fiction still echo the attitude that war is hell but provides intense moments of excitement. This attitude comes partly from a failure to understand the nature of battle. *The Wars* is a example of this. The war setting "appears almost as a gratuitous extra, a vaguely glamorous and emotive background to the torments of the young man." Descriptions of battle read "like a second-rate official history."

D44 Moss, John. Rev. of *The Wars*. In his *A Reader's Guide to the Canadian Novel*. Toronto: McClelland and Stewart, 1981, pp. 75-77. Rpt. (revised and expanded — "Timothy Findley"). 2nd ed. Toronto: McClelland and Stewart, 1987, pp. 108-18.

There is a lot wrong with *The Wars*, but it is "powerfully affecting." No one has so vividly portrayed the terrors of the battlefield. Findley deals with "great and complex moral themes," but they never resolve into a coherent structure. The reader follows the themes and events from a distance; this "dissipates the narrative energy." It is questionable whether this effect serves the novel's aspirations. Findley has a morbid fascination with homosexuality, a naïve fascination with wealth, and an "alarming and contextually appropriate interest in mutilation and brutality." *The Wars* is an "uneven achievement," but as a "rendering of conflict and the human spirit, it is superbly moving." The revised reprint is part of a longer article on Findley (C141).

D45   Beatty, Jack. Rev. of *The Wars*. *The New Republic* [Washington, D.C.], 28 March 1983, p. 36.

Beatty describes *The Wars* as a cross between Joseph Heller's *Catch 22* and Erich Maria Remarque's *All Quiet on the Western Front*. The "all too familiar" subject matter is made new by Findley's use of "modernist techniques of narrative."

FAMOUS LAST WORDS

D46   Jackson, Marni. "The Writing on the Wall Is Never Easy to Read." *Maclean's*, 26 Oct. 1981, p. 69.

Jackson calls *Famous Last Words* Findley's "postponed first novel." Comparing the novel to a film, she says Findley spent too much time directing and not enough writing. The result is that ". . . plot . . . takes precedence over characterization, to a damaging degree." While the book raises interesting questions about the role of the writer and the nature of fascism, it does not quite work as a novel. Jackson concludes that it is "brilliantly researched, damnably clever and too damned long."

D47   Blackadar, Bruce. "Brilliant Findley Novel Is a Web of Surprises." *The Toronto Star*, 31 Oct. 1981, p. F10.

Findley employs a "mind-boggling" succession of narrative techniques, cinematic devices, and a variety of locales, mind-sets, and moods in *Famous Last Words*. It is part thriller and part horror story, but also "a meditation on history and the human soul." Findley's "lush, poetic and insinuating prose" is suited to the world he portrays. *Famous Last Words* may not be a masterpiece, but it ranks as one of the year's best novels.

D48   Buitenhuis, Peter. "Famous Last Words." *The Globe and Mail* [Toronto], 31 Oct. 1981, p. E19.

Buitenhuis writes that Findley has been "bold" in his choice of the Duke and Duchess of Windsor as characters and even bolder in choosing Mauberley as his narrator. He has "crafted this novel brilliantly to explain the Windsors and illuminate the corruption of the international aristocracy of the period." His characters, however, are cardboard, they remain masks — "unknown, unknowable." The difficulties inherent in the subject may be "insuperable," but the execution is "breathtaking."

D49 Morley, Patricia. "Fascist Inscribes Hell on Hotel Walls." *The Citizen* [Ottawa], 31 Oct. 1981, p. 47.

Through Findley's "fictional mirror," the reader sees a "surreal portrait of purgatory and hell." *Famous Last Words* has "intensity, power, sensuous immediacy and humor." Its scope is epic, its theme philosophic. Much of the novel's strength lies in the Quinn-Freyberg framing device. Findley relieves scenes of horror with "fast-paced action and baroque wit." He writes to remind us of our involvement and the cost of being human.

D50 Roberts, Paul. "Findley's Name-Dropping Epic a Major Triumph." *Quill & Quire*, Nov. 1981, p. 23.

Famous Last Words is a "landmark in Canadian literature." From the discovery of Mauberley's story on the hotel walls, the novel "takes flight in a stunning series of set pieces." Beyond the story itself, Findley's prose captures with "preternatural exactness" the mood of the time. Roberts calls the book "excessive, and mad, and marvellous, puzzling, disturbing and utterly brilliant."

D51 Gervais, Marty. "Of Fascism, Kings and Final Words." *The Windsor Star*, 14 Nov. 1981, p. F5.

In *Famous Last Words*, Findley "fills in the gaps of history with conjecture." The writing-on-the-wall motif is used throughout the novel in a variety of ways. Findley's "intricate and challenging" portrayal is an "impressionistic elaboration" of Ezra Pound's poem and, at a different level, another view of history.

D52 Lane, Patrick. "A Writer at the Height of His Power." *The Edmonton Journal*, 14 Nov. 1981, p. C10.

Lane describes *Famous Last Words* as a "brilliant novel" and Findley as one of our finest novelists. He has created a "marvellous and intricate" plot from a "perfect interweaving of people, places and things." Although Lane wished at times that the novel was "more understated," he "cannot praise this book enough." He lauds Findley's use of metaphors and symbols and his "brilliantly rendered" compassion and understanding.

D53 Faustmann, John. "Royal Degradation." *The Vancouver Sun*, 27 Nov. 1981, p. L38.

Faustmann finds a "brittle beauty" in *Famous Last Words*. It is a "flight of pure imagination," a "fictional meditation" on Ezra Pound's poem. Faustmann admires Findley's ability to capture the literary style of the 1930s, but feels that the novel bogs down when he describes, "with more detail than anyone could possibly care for," the relationship of the Duke and Duchess. Mauberley's morals and politics are doubtful, and, "in a most brilliant way," Findley gives us a "peek at the beast." We cannot forgive Mauberley, but we cannot forget him.

D54 Schiefer, Nancy A. "Fascist High Times Brilliantly Portrayed." *The London Free Press*, 28 Nov. 1981, p. B11.
In this "astonishing new novel," Findley "brilliantly and hauntingly" portrays Europe in the 1930s with "cleverly orchestrated" flashbacks. Findley takes liberties with history, but, given already discovered facts, he may not be far off the mark. The novel is long on plot and short on characterization, although the Duke and Duchess are "riveting and totally believable." Findley's narrative skill, research, philosophical musings, and "breath-catching" prose make *Famous Last Words* the "major event of the Canadian book season."

D55 Wimhurst, David. " 'Words' Combines Fact, Fiction, Fascism." *The Gazette* [Montreal], 28 Nov. 1981, p. 54.
What makes *Famous Last Words* so interesting is not the Windsors, but Mauberley, and through him the ghost of Ezra Pound. The one disappointing thing in the novel is Findley's habit of "peering through historical keyholes" at the Windsors and writing about them "with all the finesse of an over-imaginative Hollywood scriptwriter."

D56 McLachlan, Ian. "Not the Full Smile." *Books in Canada*, Dec. 1981, pp. 9-11. Rpt. in *Contemporary Literary Criticism: Excerpts from Criticism of the Works of Today's Novelists, Poets, Playwrights, Short Story Writers, Filmmakers, and Other Creative Writers*. Ed. Jean C. Stine. Vol. xxvii. Detroit: Gale, 1984, 144-45.
In *Famous Last Words*, Findley has "reinvented" Ezra Pound's Mauberley for his own purposes. The conception is a fine one, but while Pound's relationship with his character is clear, Findley's is not, and the question of the protagonist's significance contributes to McLachlan's dissatisfaction with the novel. The book's multiple narrative threads remain fragments with no "convincingly imagined interdependence."

"Findley affords us some fascinating glimpses of the effects of political perversion; he leaves the causes hidden."

D57 McGoogan, Kenneth. "Famous Last Words." *The Calgary Herald*, 5 Dec. 1981, p. F20.
Findley's choice of Mauberley as narrator is "a stroke of genius"; his having Mauberley etch his story on the hotel walls is "brilliant"; and the Quinn-Freyberg framing technique is "wonderfully resonant." The reader views Findley's subject not through the supposedly clear window of psychological realism, but through a kaleidoscope of fact and fantasy. *Famous Last Words* is "the best novel I've read this year."

D58 Howard, Kirk. "A Complex Structure." *Cross-Canada Writers' Quarterly*, 4, Nos. 2-3 (1982), 39.
Famous Last Words is "a haunting yet perplexing book." While the prose is "almost poetic in its imagery and impact," the structure is overly complex. Howard also has reservations about Findley's use of historical figures, wondering if this practice is "a fair one," especially when unfavourable portraits emerge.

D59 Cameron, Elspeth. "After the Wars." *Saturday Night*, Jan. 1982, pp. 53-54. Rpt. in *Contemporary Literary Criticism: Excerpts from Criticism of the Works of Today's Novelists, Poets, Playwrights, Short Story Writers, Filmmakers, and Other Creative Writers*. Ed. Jean C. Stine. Vol. XXVII. Detroit: Gale, 1984, 145.
Famous Last Words is "a 'prose cinema' of dazzling brilliance." Following the intricate and dream-like events of Mauberley's involvement with the cabal is "like watching a spell-binding film." Like *The Wars*, the story revolves around a man trapped in wartime events, but in this novel Findley "probes the meaning of history with such insight and skill that *Famous Last Words* becomes a leap forward in his work." Cameron praises Findley's "uncanny descriptive powers" as he moves outward from a factual base to "convey an atmosphere in which the 'porcelain revery' of Pound's Mauberley poems is finally shattered . . . ." Findley recreates history "in terms that bring it uncomfortably close to us."

D60 Schieder, Rupert. "Irritating and Fascinating." *The Canadian Forum*, Feb. 1982, pp. 36-37.

Despite the complex shifts in time, point of view, and style, Schieder found himself "caught by a combination of the irritating and the fascinating" in *Famous Last Words*. The book's quotations from Ezra Pound and other writers suggest Findley's stated purpose: to search for the seeds of fascism. The Quinn-Freyberg framing device is effective, but it "complicates the problem of the fact/fiction borderline . . . ." Some readers may object to the novel's "continual sensationalism," but it reflects the world that Findley has used to embody his universal theme. Although Findley has not solved all of the problems inherent in his method and material, ". . . he has certainly succeeded in brilliantly presenting the details of this interlocking, circumscribed world . . . ."

D61 Flood, Gerald. "A Remarkable Confession." *Winnipeg Free Press*, 6 Feb. 1982, "Leisure," p. 5.

Famous Last Words is an "extraordinary book, stuffed with insights and literary surprises." Flood discusses the Quinn-Freyberg framing device and calls Quinn the "hook on which Findley snags his readers." Like Quinn, we get lost in the sensational nature of the narrative and lose sight of its objective. This "cleverly conceived" and "beautifully written" book becomes muddled in the telling of tales and loses its initial promise to weigh the morality of "superior beings."

D62 Garebian, Keith. Rev. of *Famous Last Words*. *Quarry* [30th Anniversary Issue], 31, No. 3 (Summer 1982), 93-97.

The "peculiar structure and movement" of *Famous Last Words* owe as much to the central character's "unassertive and indistinct personality" as to Findley's vision of history. It is not Mauberley who takes centre stage, but "the grimacing age itself . . . ." Findley demonstrates the pretence, self-indulgence, and emptiness of that time through theatrical metaphors and "lurid flourishes." The novel is a "beautifully haunting triumph of fiction over historical fact." It gives us an image of "an age that demands one."

D63 Hoy, Helen. "Letters in Canada: 1981. Fiction." *University of Toronto Quarterly*, 51 (Summer 1982), 332-33.

Findley's choice of Ezra Pound's Mauberley as his protagonist is "an audacious attempt to expose us to one more unsettling encounter between tradition and the individual talent, to provide another subtext for future readings of Pound." To "compound his daring," Findley attempts to elicit our sympathy for a protagonist who collaborates with fascists. *Famous Last Words* indulges too much in the drama of plots and counterplots. Findley goes beyond the "cautious invention" of historical fiction to make his historical figures into fully developed fictional characters. The novel would be tighter if Findley had relied more on "evocative glimpses of character" and less on action.

D64 Lehmann-Haupt, Christopher. Rev. of *Famous Last Words*. *The New York Times*, 22 June 1982, p. C10.

In his "remarkable new novel," Findley has mixed fact and fiction to produce a "new and bizarre form of historical romance." He has created the cabal, an ideal form of fascism, in order to recapture its appeal in the 1930s. But the cabal is the novel's weakest link, and readers will have difficulty understanding Mauberley's attraction to it. Findley creates extraordinary scenes; ". . . that such scenes . . . often veer from the plausible into the fantastic is rarely problematic and often strangely beautiful."

D65 Brennan, Anthony S. Rev. of *Famous Last Words*, by Timothy Findley; and *The Marriage Bed*, by Constance Beresford-Howe. *The Fiddlehead* [Univ. of New Brunswick], No. 133 (July 1982), pp. 82-84.

Although *Famous Last Words* is "ambitious in scope," and Findley effectively transmits the many speaking styles demanded by his characters, the novel is "an insufferable bore." It is a "mosaic of incidents" that never really comes to life. The novel's flaw is that it subjects the reader to a "heavy-sell campaign" of revelations about the conspiracy, rather than satirizing its leaders' "clownish endeavours." Since the novel's point of view is adjusted at will and is unconvincing, the reader realizes that what purports to be historical record is fiction.

D66 Strouse, Jean. "Writing on the Wall." *Newsweek* [New York], 19 July 1982, p. 67.

Contemporary authors are reversing Ezra Pound's dictum to "End fact. Try fiction," usually to the detriment of both. *Famous Last Words* is an exception. It is "a strange, brilliant weave of history and invention." Findley neither explains nor excuses his protagonist's actions, but lets the writing on the wall bear both message and judgement.

D67 Reed, J.D. "Atrocities." *Time* [New York], 2 Aug. 1982, p. 54.

Famous Last Words is ambitious and disturbing, and Findley's "most peculiar novel." Reed praises Findley's "canny" weaving of fact and fiction and his choice of Ezra Pound's character as protagonist. Mauberley "did not merely suffer from the disease of his age; he *was* the disease of his age."

D68 "Briefly Noted: Fiction." Rev. of *Famous Last Words*, by Timothy Findley; *Birds of Passage*, by Bernice Rubens; and *Satan: His Psychotherapy Cure by the Unfortunate Dr. Kassler, J.S.P.S.*, by Jeremy Leven. *The New Yorker*, 9 Aug. 1982, p. 94.

Famous Last Words is "a strange book — strange in its viewpoint, strange in its organization and in its use of real people — but it is also strangely effective . . . a very considerable accomplishment."

D69 Gold, Ivan. "Dropping Names." *The New York Times Book Review*, 15 Aug. 1982, p. 10.

Famous Last Words is "one hell of a name-dropping story" and, as in many cases involving "real" characters, the facts fit the fiction. While his prose "can turn as lush as Lawrence Durrell's . . . Mr. Findley provides relief from time to time with a zippy one-line paragraph." Gold predicts that "fictive history" will soon be out of style.

D70 Adachi, Ken. "Canadian Novels That Merit Sound of Clapping." Rev. of *Famous Last Words*, by Timothy Findley; *Bodily Harm*, by Margaret Atwood; *Riverrun*, by Peter Such; and *The Ransom Game*, by Howard Engel. *Sunday Star* [Toronto], 29 Aug. 1982, p. C10.

Within the framework of world literature, many Canadian books tend to look minor. But a few "can be categorized as superb — and the best of them deserve sustained and enthusiastic applause." Adachi quotes from favourable U.S. reviews of *Famous Last Words* as evidence of international acclaim. It "is the one novel, if you had to choose, to read this year . . . ."

D71 Benson, Eugene. " 'Whispers of Chaos': *Famous Last Words*." *World Literature Written in English* [Univ. of Guelph], 21 (Autumn 1982), 599-606.

In this review article, Benson uses the publication of *Famous Last Words* as a "convenient pretext" to review Findley's achievement of a place "in the very front ranks of contemporary novelists." Although his output is small, Findley has "written only masterpieces." Findley's one theme is violence, and in this novel he focuses on violence as it manifested itself in fascism of the 1930s. Although Findley is a political writer, his work takes on a "metaphysical cast" as he probes the nature of evil. *Famous Last Words* is an example of the "fictionalization of history." It is "so relentless and deliberate in its exploitation of history" that it is difficult to know where fact ends and fiction begins. Structurally, the novel resembles *The Last of the Crazy People* and *The Wars*, with a prologue and a series of flashbacks that reconstruct the protagonist's crime. Findley's narrative technique "continually shapes and orders." *Famous Last Words* is not only more popular than *The Wars*, it is "superior to it in craft and structure and more profound in its moral vision."

D72 Hulcoop, John F. "The Will to Be." *Canadian Literature*, No. 94 (Autumn 1982), pp. 117-22.
   Although other novelists have combined historical fact with fiction, Findley's novel is more disturbing because its protagonist compels our admiration and sympathy despite our revulsion and contempt for his fascist involvement. Findley's choice of Mauberley as narrator is "a stroke of genius." The work resembles *The Butterfly Plague* in its concern with "fascist aesthetics." *Famous Last Words* is "a brave and beautiful book": brave because Mauberley tries to tell the truth about himself and beautiful because his ambition is to describe the beautiful. Findley's "narrative facility is a marvel to behold" as he "fashions a marvellously complex 'prose kinema.' "

D73 Woodcock, George. "Recent Canadian Novels (1) Major Publishers." *Queen's Quarterly*, 89 (Winter 1982), 744, 754-59.
   Woodcock calls *Famous Last Words* "a work of great ambition whose audacities challenge one to repeated readings." It is not so much a novel as "a literary structure combining fiction, history, biography, and apocalypse." In discussing style and surface, Woodcock acknowledges not only Findley's "literary dexterity," but also the "sophistication of a literature that has come to the point where forms and artifices, parodies and pastiches, are the serious concerns of serious writers." Woodcock suggests that certain verses in Ezra Pound's poem gave Findley clues as to how Mauberley should compose his masterpiece. Findley presents us with his views on the nature and effects of war and the real character of history. The moralism "that goes with the territory of fiction" is expressed through the characters of Pound, Quinn, and Freyberg.

D74 Davenport, Gary. "Pound Foolish, Nobody Wise." *Sewanee Review* [Univ. of the South, Sewanee, Tenn.], 91, No. 1 (Jan.–March 1983), xviii–xx.

Contemporary fiction is often remarkable for its ingenuity of situation and incident, and a reader's response is either positive or negative wonder. *Famous Last Words* is an example of this tradition. The novel should have both popular and intellectual appeal, but it is essentially superficial. It tries to be several things at once: a historical thriller, social criticism, and a novel of character, but falls short even by popular standards. Most of the writing is bad, and there are "no engaging persons or ideas in it."

D75 Hair, Donald. "To Catch the Reader Unaware." *Brick* [Ilderton, Ont.], No. 17 (Winter 1983), pp. 8-14.

Famous Last Words is "a good read," appealing simply for its action, adventure, and intrigue. Hair discusses how the novel successfully portrays "the spirit of the age." The use of a *Doppelgänger* device, the myth of Narcissus, and the recurring use of mirrors suggest that Mauberley, as well as other characters and the reader, see in themselves the disease of the age. An essential feature of the novel's form is a "text which prods, challenges, stimulates, provokes." Mauberley's writing is not "the" truth, but a limited truth learned through experience and leading the reader "to the subtler and more complex truth . . . ." A double point of view is used effectively, most obviously in the differing responses of Quinn and Freyberg to Mauberley's writing. Findley's juxtaposition of the artistic and demonic world views is what places *Famous Last Words* "considerably above the usual story of intrigue . . . ."

D76 Cropper, Martin. "Through the Looking Glass." Rev. of *Famous Last Words*, by Timothy Findley; and *I the Supreme*, by Augusto Roa Bastos. *London Daily News*, 19 March 1987, "New Fiction," p. 19.

Findley's "artful thriller" is criticized for its portrayal of the Duke and Duchess of Windsor. Cropper wonders who is supposed to be narrating the passages in third person that connect the personal memoirs. They are the novel's most stimulating prose.

D77 Sinclair, Andrew. "Aunt Rose's Wild Cabin." Rev. of *Famous Last Words*, by Timothy Findley; *Dessa Rose*, by Shirley Anne Williams;

Queen of Hearts, by Susan Richards Shreve; and *Lallia: Le Cow-Boy*, by Djanet Lachmet. *The Times* [London], 19 March 1987, p. 17.

Findley's invention of the last decade of Mauberley's career is a "brilliant device."

D78   Kermode, Frank. "A Royal Coup." *The Guardian* [London], 20 March 1987, p. 13.

Kermode complains of the treatment of the Duke and Duchess of Windsor. The story is "very nearly pure tosh," in spite of "the author's command of historical detail and his fertility in the invention of suitable nasty incidents." Findley is "a literary person who can write decent prose," but who has chosen a best-seller formula.

D79   Carpenter, Humphrey. "Windsor Soup." *Observer* [London], 22 March 1987, "Arts & Books," p. 26.

While Carpenter admits that Mauberley may be a good subject for a novel, he cannot see why Findley chose him "for this particular enterprise." Unlike Ezra Pound's poet, "out of key with his time," Findley's Mauberley is a man of action who writes pro-fascist articles and is willing "to machinate on behalf of the cabal." Carpenter praises the vivid glimpse of Charles Lindbergh and how the novel "lifts off brilliantly" during the encounters between Edward VIII and Queen Mary. "Findley could have created a magnificent novel that dealt solely with the Windsors' private lives . . . ."

D80   Tonkin, Boyd. "Hitler's Understudy." *New Statesman* [London], 27 March 1987, p. 33.

Famous Last Words is "unmistakably a work of our time," because it "holds up a glass, not to the 1930s, but to the suspicion and amnesia of the Age of Reagan." It makes a fantasy of the past in the manner of Anthony Burgess's *Earthly Powers* and E.L. Doctorow's *Ragtime*. Such novels "refer not so much to a pattern of actualities as to the clutter of cultural artifacts that gather round them." Findley plays on an emotion unique to this century — "heart-stopping nostalgia for a world we never knew."

D81   Gill, John. "The King and I." *Time Out* [London], 25 March–1 April 1987, p. 28.

Famous Last Words is "an engrossing but plausible story about contingency alliances and everyday evil." Findley is shocked by the suggestion that he is putting forward the conspiracy theory as fact. The circumstances of the story are secondary to its moral considerations.

D82   Stewart, Ian. "Four Novel Interpretations of Real Life." Rev. of *Change*, by Maureen Duffy; *Famous Last Words*, by Timothy Findley; *To Kill a God*, by Paul Rodgers; and *The Memoirs of Christopher Columbus*, by Stephen Marlowe. *Illustrated London News*, April 1987, p. 68.

Stewart suggests that Findley's "name-dropping extravagance" may not be to everyone's taste, but praises the novel's narrative technique, "moving confidently about in time and space." More stimulating than the "gossipy if colourful interest" of many of the novel's episodes is its "strand of reflective commentary . . . with its insights into the corruption of mind and spirit in a disintegrating world."

D83   Reynolds, Stanley. "Cold Comfort Melvyn." Rev. of *The Maid of Buttermere*, by Melvyn Bragg; and *Famous Last Words*, by Timothy Findley. *Punch* [London], 8 April 1987, p. 59.

Reynolds disagrees with reviewers in the U.S. and Canada who call *Famous Last Words* a masterpiece. Findley cannot sustain the necessary "haughty Edwardian lingo" and one can "see the joins where fact meets fiction." Reynolds concludes that ". . . there really should be some law to protect people like the late Duchess from books like this."

D84   Melmoth, John. "The Off-the-Wall Writing on the Wall." *TLS: The Times Literary Supplement* [London], 24 April 1987, p. 435.

Melmoth discusses Mauberley's and Ezra Pound's collusions with fascism and suggests that while Findley explores his protagonist's motives and guilt, he fails to come to any satisfactory conclusions. Because Freyberg's judgement is questioned, "Findley ducks the most important issue that his novel raises." The narrative is "sophisticated and intriguing . . . full of quirks and surprises." As alternative history, however, ". . . it is pleasantly scabrous and spiteful but never convincing."

D85   Turgeon, Pierre. "L'histoire, vrai ou faux?". Rev. of *Le Grand Elysium Hotel*, by Timothy Findley, trans. Bernard Géniès; and *Le Tennis de Alfonce*, by James Petrick Donleavy. *L'Actualité*, 12 (mai 1987), 162, 164.

Turgeon puts forth the hypothesis that history texts are really novels, based on a mixture of truth and fiction, set up as truth to serve the interests of those in power. This allows Findley to take any liberties he wants with historical events. He so skillfully mixes fiction and reality that the reader slides little by little into a troubled universe where anything is possible. The historical figures drift in a labyrinth of mirrors where the reader can admire their reflections, deformed and multiplied by fiction. This superb novel shows us how myth is intertwined with history. In French.

DINNER ALONG THE AMAZON

D86 Manguel, Alberto. "Findley's People." *Books in Canada*, June–July 1984, pp. 13-14, 16.

The characters in this "astounding" collection of stories never question what happens to them. Instead they collect evidence about themselves, perform rituals, and devise new ways of dealing with their guilt and loneliness. Findley's people "are a conglomerate, a group functioning as one single being." The reader enters their world through the eyes of a character, or on his own with no interpreter. This world is an "excellent definition of Canada." The collection is also a "showcase of drafts, ideas, new developments, variations on the obsessions that make up Findley's chosen world."

D87 Adachi, Ken. "Findley Boom Keeps Rolling." *The Toronto Star*, 14 July 1984, "Books," p. M4.

Works from different periods collected together entail a risk, but Findley "survives the ordeal of retrospection quite adroitly." There is in his work a "distinctive structural and symbolic unity" that comes from themes of loneliness and longing, guilt and regret. The detail in his prose provides dense patterns of imagery, but there is "something disconcerting in the way his realism suddenly becomes surreal." Findley's accomplishments with the short story are "as solid as they are brilliant."

D88 French, William. "Too Much Betrayal." *The Globe and Mail* [Toronto], 14 July 1984, p. 15.

Dinner Along the Amazon allows us to trace Findley's development and preoccupations over the 30 years the stories span. Betrayal is a recurring theme. The later stories emphasize relationships, rather than a strong story line, and portray a bleak view of life. The earlier stories are more attractive. Even when innocence is betrayed, it is acceptable as part of the process of growing up. These stories demonstrate Findley's facility with dialogue and his ability "to create a compelling aura of mystery and strong sense of mood and place."

D89 Percy, H.R. "Along Findley's Amazon a Jungle of Despair." *Quill & Quire*, Aug. 1984, p. 30.

The world of Findley's stories is a "great place to visit but you wouldn't want to live there." It is a world where no one is happy for long and "doom or disillusionment is presaged from the first page." But the best of the stories allow us to rise above the anguish and futility and are "transmuted by the leaven of language into something fine and highly enjoyable . . . ." In "Lemonade," Findley displays profound insight into a child's mind. "Dinner Along the Amazon" is the "ultimate triumph," culminating in a brilliant monologue.

D90 Ibsen, Joy. "A Rare Literary Breed Gains Recognition in Canada." Rev. of *The Thrill of the Grass*, by W.P. Kinsella; *Dinner Along the Amazon*, by Timothy Findley; *Melancholy Elephants*, by Spider Robinson; *Champagne Barn*, by Norman Levine; and *The Pool in the Desert*, by Sara Jeannette Duncan. *The London Free Press*, 31 Aug. 1984, p. A13.

Ibsen notes that four of the early stories in *Dinner Along the Amazon* share the common theme of a boy feeling hurt by his family's isolation. Later stories are more complex, dealing with relationships, marriages, obsessions, and latent homosexuality.

D91 Dawe, Alan. "Short Fiction: The Gentle Art." Rev. of *Dinner Along the Amazon*, by Timothy Findley; and *The Thrill of the Grass*, by W.P. Kinsella. *The Vancouver Sun*, 15 Sept. 1984, "Books," p. C14.

The stories in *Dinner Along the Amazon* are "distinguished, on the one hand, by Findley's clean, elegant style and, on the other, by the uniformly depressing lives of his characters." These stories "are not only memorable and varied fictions, they also provide a fascinating study" of how Findley has developed his distinctive style.

D92 Rooke, Constance. Rev. of *Dinner Along the Amazon*. *The Malahat Review* [Univ. of Victoria], No. 69 (Oct. 1984), p. 120.

Rooke finds much to admire in this collection, but her response is cool. "Lemonade" is the best story. "Many of the other, complex fictions here display Findley's talents without quite achieving that cohesive play of the imagination that makes a world . . . ."

D93 Cornish, Mary Lou. "The Presence of Fear." *Cross-Canada Writers' Quarterly*, 7, Nos. 3-4 (1985), 43-44.

In this collection of "finely-crafted" stories, Findley displays a wide range of themes and styles. A "strong and undeniable presence of fear" links the stories that are both appealing and unsettling. Findley's believable and vulnerable characters make the stories mesmerizing. He writes visually, but not cinematically, more like a still-life painter.

D94 Gabriel, Barbara. Rev. of *Dinner Along the Amazon*. *Canadian Fiction Magazine*, No. 54 (1985), pp. 87-89.

The themes that dominate Findley's major fiction can be found in the stories of this collection, but one theme emerges more clearly than ever before — that of sexual politics. "Consistently in these stories, it is men, betrayed by their own myths of maleness, who, in turn, destroy women." In "Sometime — Later — Not Now," one of the best stories in the collection, the politics of sex relate not only to the connection between war and the myth of maleness, but to a "sensitive and radical interpretation of the heroine's whole life."

D95 Murray, Rona. Rev. of *It Never Pays to Laugh Too Much*, by Gertrude Story; *Out on the Plain*, by Frankie Finn; and *Dinner Along the Amazon*, by Timothy Findley. *Event*, 14, No. 2 (1985), 145-46.

One fascinating aspect of this collection is that we can trace in it the development of Findley's writing skills. We also become aware of the repetitions in his imagery and subject matter. "The same voice speaks throughout. The voice becomes surer of itself." In the later stories, "more is hinted, more is left to the reader's imagination . . . ." It is a "sad and unsettling book. It's also absorbing."

D96 Woodcock, George. "The Dimming of Innocence." *Canadian Literature*, No. 104 (Spring 1985), pp. 140-41.

In Findley's stories we find both "patiently perfected prose" and an "imaginative authenticity that irradiates everything he writes . . . ." Woodcock divides the stories into two groups: those about childhood innocence and those about the "collective falsehoods of experience" in adult life. Counterbalancing the childhood stories of destroyed innocence are a few "strangely joyful tales of beings whose essential innocence is invulnerable." In the adult stories, artifice is most obviously displayed and, at times imagination wavers before the brilliance of invention.

D97 Levene, Mark. "Letters in Canada: 1984. Fiction: 2." *University of Toronto Quarterly*, 54 (Summer 1985), 328-30.

In "the most complex and powerful collection of stories published this year," Findley explores the "inevitability of loss and the constant silence at the heart of all life." Findley's "imagistic, almost hallucinatory" language is at odds with the rambling shape of some of the stories. One of his most striking techniques is to have the narrator define how much the character says and how much he keeps silent, a perfect mirror of experience. "Dinner Along the Amazon" is an example of Findley's art "at its most commanding." The story's "nuances of feeling are palpable."

D98 Thompson, Eric. "Let Us Compare Obsessions." Rev. of *Champagne Barn*, by Norman Levine; and *Dinner Along the Amazon*, by Timothy Findley. *The Fiddlehead* [Univ. of New Brunswick], No. 145 (Autumn 1985), pp. 104-05.

In the Introduction to *Dinner Along the Amazon*, Findley discusses how his obsessions have inspired his fiction. His most obvious obsession and "metaphor for madness," is war; another is loneliness. Both can be found in these stories. Findley's world of illusion is disturbing, dominated by "various kinds of madness or perversion." His most substantial achievement in form is "Hello Cheeverland, Goodbye."

NOT WANTED ON THE VOYAGE

D99 Hill, Douglas. "Apocalypse Then." *Books in Canada*, Nov. 1984, pp. 11-12.

In *Not Wanted on the Voyage*, Findley "reframes a myth and sails through and beyond it, into a daring and sustained flight of timely philosophical significance." A number of things contribute to the story's strength: the "believability" and "sheer humanness" of the characters; an empathy with animals that is charming, poignant, and profound; and prose that is rich in idiom, rhythms, and cadences and mixes styles and tones. Findley's vision is "apocalyptic."

D100 Manguel, Alberto. "Timothy Findley's Masterful Journey on Noah's Ark." *Quill & Quire*, Nov. 1984, p. 34.

Findley has ignored the tradition of "timorous literary theology and has given us a God with both feet firmly planted on our Earth." He has chosen to work against the reader's expectations to create "the backstage of the Bible." Others have written of the flood, but have not explored the story for its own sake. Each character has a secret and the revelations of these secrets are the threads of the intricate plot. Findley's theme is a "concern for the individual's uniqueness, and a belief in the individual's free will."

D101 Adachi, Ken. "An Ark Jammed with Treasures." *The Toronto Star*, 3 Nov. 1984, "Books," p. M4.

Each of Findley's novels has been "surprising, a departure achieved after considerable contemplative effort and calculation of risk." *Not Wanted on the Voyage* is no exception, and it is a success. Its "deliberately planted anachronisms" help the novel become a story, not just about the past, but about the present and the future — "a mammoth statement on good and evil." What begins as a fable about survival is, like Findley's other novels, transformed into a study of isolation.

D102 Ackerman, Marianne. "Findley Spins Magical Tale With 'New' Noah." *The Gazette* [Montreal], 10 Nov. 1984, p. I1.

In this "audacious retelling" of the Noah story, Findley shifts the narrative point of view in order to attack our civilization's "warrior impulse," an impulse which denies the feminine, excludes the handicapped, and glorifies the powerful. The novel is an "amazing feat of imagination," "splendidly structured," with characters who are "absorbing and real." Rather than trivializing a sacred story, Findley's account "pays homage to an enduring myth."

D103 Abley, Mark. "The Cat and Noah's Ark." *Maclean's*, 12 Nov. 1984, p. 64a.

For "sheer bravado," *Not Wanted on the Voyage* is unmatched, but Findley's reach exceeds his grasp. In this "witty, sombre" retelling of the story of Noah, Findley has adapted a scriptural tale to convey contemporary messages of social and political warning. Yet, the novel is "only a qualified success." It is "the strangest novel to appear this year."

D104 Goodden, Herman. "A Brilliant, Blasphemous Replay of Noah and the Flood." *The London Free Press*, 23 Nov. 1984, p. A15.

Findley examines the story of Noah "with fresh eyes" to show ". . . it wasn't like that." The sense of "omniverous doom" in his earlier work is "deepened and darkened" in this novel. Findley's characters are convincing, "drawn in broad, elemental strokes," and he handles fantastic elements with an effective "bald-faced" approach. The reader is forced to see the old story in a new way through Findley's "crazy, brilliant, blasphemous" interpretation.

D105 French, William. "Biblical Science Fiction." *The Globe and Mail* [Toronto], 24 Nov. 1984, "Books," p. 19.

Not Wanted on the Voyage is a "work of considerable imagination and daring." It is more fantasy than allegory and readers who do not have the necessary suspension of disbelief will regard it as "Biblical science fiction." Findley's ark is "freighted with a heavy cargo of symbolism" to convey several messages: equality for women, the need for conservation, the threat posed by fundamentalists, and the danger of unquestioning belief. The transformation of Lucifer into a compassionate character, and Noah into an evil one, is Findley's comment on "the slippery nature of good and evil."

D106 Gray-Grant, Daphne. "Back to the Ark in a Blinding Flash . . . ." *The Vancouver Sun*, 27 Nov. 1984, p. C1.

Findley admits *Not Wanted on the Voyage* is a "daring" book that may anger religious fundamentalists and confuse readers who expect another novel like *The Wars*. The book is "neither bitter nor smug." It is "warm and surprisingly believable," with a fine blend of the fantastic and the horrible.

D107 McGoogan, Kenneth. "Findley Gambles on Noah." *Calgary Herald*, 9 Dec. 1984, p. F8.

McGoogan relates the origins of *Not Wanted on the Voyage* — how Findley began writing about his blind cat but changed direction after hearing a Phyllis Webb poem. While "no novelist in Canada rivals Findley for sheer imaginative power," and the novel is "brilliant in its parts," it lacks a coherent vision. McGoogan recommends the novel for "its flashes of greatness."

D108 Cude, Wilfred. "It Wasn't Like That." *The Antigonish Review* [St. Francis Xavier Univ.], No. 60 (Winter 1985), pp. 95-99.

Not Wanted on the Voyage is a "fine and sophisticated refashioning of one of humanity's more appalling stories into a cautionary fable for our time." The essence of this fable, and "moral climax of the novel," is the conflict between Noah's denial and Mrs. Noye's affirmation of the sanctity of life. In *Not Wanted on the Voyage*, we find many of Findley's "obsessions": the handicapped as spiritual link between human and animal, the death of a child by fascist thugs, and animals sacrificed to human pride. This novel is "one of the most intriguing patterns yet formulated in the kaleidoscope of Findley's imagination."

D109 Fitzgerald, Judith. "Noah's Patriarchy." *The Canadian Forum*, Feb. 1985, pp. 36-37.

Findley's "near-fastidious attention to form, craft, and content" may allow him to become Canada's first Nobel Prize winner for literature. *Not Wanted on the Voyage* is informed with Findley's consistent vision of "the perils of being human, the perils of human beings." The fable is built on Arnold Toynbee's idea that the essential holiness of all things lost its power with the acceptance of monotheism. Findley's portrayal of "compassionate animals and careless humans" emphasizes an idea that is central to his message. His "allegorical warning of impending holocaust is urgent and devastating."

D110 Rooke, Constance. "Books in Review: Fiction." *The Malahat Review* [Univ. of Victoria], No. 70 (March 1985), pp. 158-59.

Not Wanted on the Voyage is a "rich, engaging, and ambitious novel." It is structured around a feminist analysis of myth and history, but Findley "mixes things up" so that the female principle is not entirely pure, the men are not all villains, and there are numerous gender-crossings. It is an "idealistic book that is wary of idealism . . . pessimistic . . . but . . . loving; above all, it is *humane*."

D111 Harrison, James. Rev. of *Not Wanted on the Voyage*. *World Literature Written in English* [Univ. of Guelph], 25 (Spring 1985), 118-20.

In *Not Wanted on the Voyage*, Findley has dispensed with the "authenticating narrative frames" and "documentary format" of his earlier novels and has chosen an "easy omniscience which flows in and out of sundry centres of consciousness . . . ." Credibility is bypassed and, at the same time, established by the use of one family to represent all of humanity. The arc of the narrative is parabolic, "veering towards and then away from the axis of allegory, and refusing to be pinned down to a moral." The novel's "richly and complexly imagined world" is far removed from "simplistic diagrams of allegory and fable," yet it has a "single-minded, compelling force . . . ."

D112 Levene, Mark. "Letters in Canada: 1984. Fiction: 2." *University of Toronto Quarterly*, 54 (Summer 1985), 330-32.

Every "magnificent" detail in Findley's novel is "intrinsic to this lyrical, funny, and brutal story of the unending battle between fanaticism and compassion." Mrs. Noyes struggles against her husband's instinct to destroy; her instinct is to give sanctuary, to maintain life. Findley "never falters in modulating her voice and stature." Lucy is the novel's "most extraordinary achievement." Like Lucy, the animals in the novel represent an "amazing leap of the imagination." Findley maintains the most effective distance between the reader and his mythical subject by knowing "when to assert and when to withdraw modern phrasing and rhythms." More importantly, he knows how "to make beauty seem slightly alien . . . ."

D113 Fuller, Edmund. "Ark of Triumph." *The Wall Street Journal* [New York], 10 Sept. 1985, p. 28.

Not Wanted on the Voyage is "remarkable for style and imagination," but Fuller has "no good words" for its philosophy and theology. Yahweh could not have been "self-revivified" since he is the Old Testament God with no possibility of resurrection. Nor does he even notice Noah's sins of lust, cruelty, and fornication. Although Findley likes Lucy very much, Fuller does not. The novel does have several "triumphantly successful" characters who lift "our spirits on the voyage" but cannot "eliminate the underlying bleakness of Mr. Findley's vision."

D114 Barbour, Douglas. "Mythic-Comic Opera." *Canadian Literature*, No. 106 (Fall 1985), pp. 161-63.

Not Wanted on the Voyage is a "wondrous, if terrifically dark, visionary text." One of the most interesting aspects of reading this book is "watching the text struggle" with the limitations of the fable to express philosophical, psychological, and theological complexities. Through the perception of Mottyl, Findley brings the natural world to life. The novel reads like a "kind of *The Wind in the Willows*, with people." He successfully blends "the mythic and the comic opera" elements in the novel. All fables have morals, "but few present theirs with as much energy and imaginative power" as Findley's.

D115 Keith, W.J. Rev. of *Not Wanted on the Voyage*. *The Fiddlehead* [Univ. of New Brunswick], No. 145 (Autumn 1985), pp. 82-84.

Not Wanted on the Voyage is both a "brilliant reexamination of Timothy Findley's recurring concerns and a dazzling advance into new imaginative territory." Findley "revels in jolting us with anachronisms" that reveal themselves to be the whole point of the novel. That Yahweh is dead and Noah asserts mastery over humans and nature comes "close to the heart of Findley's meaning." *Not Wanted on the Voyage* is a profoundly feminist novel, but that does not mean Findley panders to the "fashionable crusades of our times." Findley is a "major imaginative artist" who would not be comfortable "in a world which he considers dangerously unimaginative."

D116 Raphael, Isabel. "Tiresome Women, Transatlantic Tales." Rev. of *Men and Angels*, by Mary Gordon; and *Not Wanted on the Voyage*, by Timothy Findley. *The Times* [London], 31 Oct. 1985, p. 12.

Despite the optimism of the traditional Noah and the ark story, *Not Wanted on the Voyage* is "a very angry book" that deals with exploitation and devastation. Findley's writing is "surprisingly consistent" and, after a slow start, "gains urgency." This novel could become a "cult book," especially in Canada.

D117 Fothergill, Robert A. "After the Deluge . . . ." *TLS: The Times Literary Supplement* [London], 1 Nov. 1985, p. 1228.

Findley reads the story of Noah very differently than the traditional interpretations, and Fothergill can only agree with him. Before the narrative has time to "override the prototype," the reader is uncertain of Noah's moral worth, but with the onset of the flood he emerges as "increasingly fanatical and frantic." Lucy is "one of the book's most remarkable inventions." If Findley's writing is to be faulted, it would be for a tendency to "overplay the whimsy to the point of cuteness" and a gratuitous piling on of horrors. Findley's fiction has always been preoccupied with the "qualities of innocence and the sources of malignity."

D118 Hill, Douglas. "Bold Experiments." Rev. of *Not Wanted on the Voyage*, by Timothy Findley; *Soldiers' Pay*, by William Faulkner;

Mosquitoes, by William Faulkner; and *The Ink Truck*, by William Kennedy. *The Globe and Mail* [Toronto], 2 Nov. 1985, p. D19.

Hill reviews four novels that "experiment boldly with form and language." Only *Not Wanted on the Voyage* deserves to be called a masterpiece. It is "no less than a book of wonders" with "fully fleshed, petty and grand, above all eloquent" characters. Findley has turned the flood myth into a metaphor for our own precarious times.

D119 McCorkle, Jill. "Genesis Meets Tobacco Road." *The New York Times Book Review*, 10 Nov. 1985, p. 14G.

Findley's complex and highly imaginative tale accurately depicts human nature and emotions with "a cast of characters rich and imaginative enough to persuade the reader to suspend his disbelief." The reader is "initially distracted" by Mottyl the cat, but she wins our affections and proves to be the true voice of the novel.

D120 Manguel, Alberto. "Timothy Findley's Rain of Terror." *The Village Voice* [New York], 29 April 1986, pp. 47-48.

Like Findley's earlier works, *Not Wanted on the Voyage* explores the theme of "the human animal and the world it destroys." Findley is a "moralist-storyteller" who is saying that in a world of destruction where creation is a crime, "both artist and dreamer are punished." He recognizes human isolation but does not allow his characters to give in. "Mrs. Noyes and Mottyl are a universal memory that prevents the annihilation" of life. Mottyl is one of Findley's most memorable characters — she "is neither a symbol nor a human in cat's clothing . . . no small literary triumph." Findley's work is the exception to Northrop Frye's assertion that Canada has no great classic writers.

THE TELLING OF LIES

D121 Schiefer, Nancy A. "Symbolic Comment on Clash of Two Centuries." *The London Free Press*, 24 Oct. 1986, p. A19.

The Telling of Lies is "a compulsive page-turner," a success as a mystery, but it is also a very political novel. Like Margaret Atwood's *The Handmaid's Tale*, it is a cautionary tale in its comments on the United States and Canada — "their values, their vagaries, the pipers they choose to follow." Findley is "superb" with detail, especially in his depiction of the resort hotel, but "less subtle" in depicting the political overtones of the story.

D122 Adachi, Ken. "Lies and Secrets Hiding Inside Family Relations." *The Toronto Star*, 25 Oct. 1986, "Books," p. M4.

At the core of this novel are the "lies and secrets endemic in family relations and society at large." Findley has found a setting and protagonist that allows him "to exploit some of his favorite techniques and explore some of his favorite themes." The novel becomes a kind of prism "refracting social, political and intellectual values." Moments of "superb satire" are sometimes achieved at the expense of the characters "who tend to become fuzzy cartoon figures, representative of a given moral or ideological stance." The iceberg does not really work, but Adachi forgives Findley for "his playful indulgence."

D123 Cannon, Margaret. "The Refined Art of a Story-Teller." *The Globe and Mail* [Toronto], 25 Oct. 1986, p. E19.

Findley is "one of the world's great story-tellers, and in *The Telling of Lies* he has a marvellous tale to tell." He has a gift for settings, and the hotel is a "perfect background" for the story. The plot is complicated and occasionally gets tangled. Findley pushes the literary message a bit too hard and is not totally at home with the mystery form, but these are minor flaws in a "marvellous" book. It is both a novel about great wickedness and a "page-flipping whodunnit."

D124 Yanofsky, Joel. "Timothy Findley's Whodunit Is Medium for His Message." *The Gazette* [Montreal], 25 Oct. 1986, p. B8.

The Telling of Lies is a "hybrid" — a mystery that relies more on atmosphere and characterization than plot. Its characters owe more to Anton Chekhov than to mystery writers. This "clash of style and story" worked better in Findley's earlier novels. The "graceful cynicism of Findley's writing and the curious characters" are overshadowed by a contrived ending. Findley's style has changed, but his message remains the same: "the corrupt alliance . . . between evil and complacency."

D125 Grady, Wayne. "Sharing the Guilt." *Books in Canada*, Nov. 1986, pp. 16-17.

Findley is concerned not so much with solving mysteries as with studying the effects of mysteries on those involved in them. *The Telling of Lies* is a "prison novel, a study of the psychology of the suspects." This explains the presence of the "not very successfully integrated" sections on Vanessa's childhood experience in a Japanese detention camp. It is an odd mystery, and there is a temptation to "credit its inconclusiveness and oddity to its being a grab-bag of discarded Findleyana over which a tea-cosy of detective fiction has been superimposed." But its oddity and inconclusiveness make it an "ideal simulacrum of real life."

D126 Roberts, Paul. "Findley's Lies Much More Than a Mystery." *Quill & Quire*, Nov. 1986, p. 22.

Findley turns the mystery genre "on its head." The issue of why Maddox was killed ultimately dominates the book, overriding the crime and the identity of the criminal. Although it has a less panoramic sweep than *Famous Last Words* or *Not Wanted on the Voyage*, this novel deals with the same theme of "the infamies of this century." *The Telling of Lies* is "an anguished reminder of man's lack of humanity, and of the responsibility to be vigilant and compassionate in the face of this knowledge." The novel is "a rare, beautiful, moving work . . . the best thing I have read this year."

D127 Henderson, Heather. "Strangers on the Shore." *Maclean's*, 3 Nov. 1986, p. 66b.

Findley has "deftly assembled all the paraphernalia of the classic whodunit," but the familiar form crumbles under the weight of his "bleak moral vision." The novel comes from the twentieth-century nightmare of man's capacity to destroy not only bodies, but souls. *The Telling of Lies* loses its early intensity after Maddox's death and "lacks the poetic energy needed to fuse its bleak imagery and vision with action."

D128 Moreira, Peter. "Mystery Findley's Obvious Genre." *The Chronicle-Herald* [Halifax], 8 Nov. 1986, p. 27.

The mystery is an obvious genre for Findley, whose books often "start with an inexplicable situation and gradually reveal why and how the situation occurred." "His craft as a mystery writer is flawed only by his refusal to give the reader a fair chance to solve the mystery . . . his strength as a novelist is shown in the humanity he has injected into a whodunnit."

D129 Sigurdson, Norman. "A Meditation on Deception." *Winnipeg Free Press*, 8 Nov. 1986, p. 79.

"Findley seems to have hit upon a structure and a genre which suit his particular talent for vivid scene-setting." He is a highly descriptive writer and his rendering of the hotel guests is delightful. Vanessa is a "remarkable creation." Unfortunately, the characters are "locked into a plot which becomes increasingly absurd . . . ." Findley is "fatally attracted to excess." *The Telling of Lies* rises above its flaws to "provide an entertaining and often quite humorous meditation on deception."

D130 Van Herk, Aritha. "Mystery Novel's Political Subplot Blurs Its Strength." *Calgary Herald*, 17 Nov. 1986, p. C1.

The mystery in *The Telling of Lies* is never fully explained, but Findley's "ability to unfold a tale both translucent and opaque is further consolidated" in this novel. Vanessa is an "unqualified success" as a narrator and the device of having a photographer record what is omitted is perfect for a mystery novel. The prison camp scenes are a "haunting counterpoint to the images of submersion in the present-day story." When the story shifts to politics, however, ". . . the imagistic effect blurs." The novel is "superb in its evocation and brilliant in its masterful writing."

D131 Cude, Wilfred. Rev. of *The Telling of Lies*. *The Antigonish Review* [St. Francis Xavier Univ.], No. 68 (1987), pp. 55-60.

Findley's novel is a "whodunit," but its thematic structure "brings the reader instantly to some of the most challenging ethical, political and cultural issues of our place in history" and dramatizes important issues that have been ignored or trivialized. "Poignant cultural clashes, prominent and colorful symbols, and unmistakable allusions" make Findley's intent and meaning clear. Cude discusses the importance of the Japanese prison camp and the iceberg in the novel, as well as Canadian readers' reactions. Findley warns us that because we are blind to the "faces of human monstrosity," we think it cannot happen here. Through Vanessa, he cautions us against "tolerating abuses of institutional power in the name of patriotism."

D132 Jackson, Marni. "Findley Delves Into Deceit and Death." Rev. of *The Telling of Lies*, by Timothy Findley; *A Misalliance*, by Anita Brookner; *Joe & Marilyn: A Memory of Love*, by Roger Kahn; and *The Fitzgeralds and the Kennedys*, by Doris Kearns. *Chatelaine*, Jan. 1987, p. 8.

Jackson praises the details in *The Telling of Lies* but finds the plot too clever in spots. "If there's sometimes too much palaver in Findley's prose, the risks he takes pay off."

D133 Levene, Mark. "Letters in Canada: 1986. Fiction: 2." *University of Toronto Quarterly*, 57 (Fall 1987), 17-18.
Levene finds in Findley's "first formal mystery" a number of "superb sequences," including descriptions of the iceberg and the beach and Vanessa's memories of her family's imprisonment. Findley's "unnerving gift for layering the real and the surreal, for revealing primal impulses beneath the intricacies of social experience," is evident throughout. He is less successful in reconciling the different narrative types upon which he draws, chiefly because of "the awkwardness of his plotting." Vanessa details the characters of her old friends with precision and sympathy, but Findley does not allow her awareness to extend to the novel's villains, who "seem to be on loan and on the prowl for the foreground of another narrative."

D134 Hutcheon, Linda. "Murder & Lies." Rev. of *A Single Death*, by Eric Wright; and *The Telling of Lies*, by Timothy Findley. *Canadian Literature*, No. 115 (Winter 1987), pp. 225-27.
The Telling of Lies is a "self-reflexive, metafictional kind of mystery." The mystery form is a "readily recognized way of signalling to the reader the . . . fictionality of what she is reading." In Findley's morally ambiguous world, where the past always conditions the present, to lie is to fictionalize. Vanessa is an unwilling detective and an unwilling writer, "who distrusts language, while acknowledging her reliance upon it."

D135 Ellmann, Lucy. "Duck Soup." Rev. of *Cutting Timber*, by Thomas Bernhard; *Little Misunderstandings of No Importance*, by Antonio Tabucchi; *Burning Patience*, by Antonio Skarmeta; and *The Telling of Lies*, by Timothy Findley. *The Guardian* [London], 25 March 1988, p. 27.
The novel's "pallid protagonists," "mild, long-winded expression of ambivalence towards the C.I.A.," and "dull diary" format do not make "a very suspenseful unravelling of what purports to be a murder mystery." The only thing mysterious about the novel is why Findley wrote it.

D136 Dalley, Jan. "The Avon Lady Calls." Rev. of *The Mermaids*, by Patty Dann; *Stop House Blues*, by Maggie Hemingway; *The Telling of Lies*, by Timothy Findley; and *Small Tales of a Town*, by Susan Webster. *Sunday Observer* [London], 27 March 1988, p. 42.

Dalley focuses on the symbolism of the novel's iceberg. The device, an attempt to "adopt a veneer of symbolic chic," does not work. Nor is Vanessa's "unifying presence" sufficient to give the novel coherence.

D137 Melmoth, John. "Sleuthing in Sepia Tints." *TLS: The Times Literary Supplement* [London], 15-21 April 1988, p. 421.

The Telling of Lies "suffers from not being sure precisely what sort of thing it is." It tries to be more than a routine "twinset-and-dagger thriller," but ends up being something less than a serious novel. The narrator Vanessa is unsuited to the job of investigating a murder, but Findley does not take advantage of the fictional possibilities in the disjunction between a voice and what it has to tell. His preoccupation with Vanessa's world — the world of the Aurora Sands Hotel — distracts him from the harsher realities of life. Melmoth concludes that ". . . what is apparently intended to be a witty and sophisticated fusion of political thriller and epistemological novel, capable of making capital of the narrator's limitations, emerges as neither one thing nor the other."

D138 Sullivan, Jack. Rev. of *The Telling of Lies*, by Timothy Findley. *The New York Times Book Review*, 9 Oct. 1988, p. 34.

In *The Last of the Crazy People*, Findley displayed his skill in using a crime story as the nucleus of a serious book; he does so again in *The Telling of Lies*. Sullivan comments on Findley's atmospheric setting and vividly drawn narrator and calls it "a novel of charm and manners, if of a rather chilly sort." Findley's "delicate balancing act" is reinforced by the perceptions of his heroine, who sees "intricate symmetries" in her story. Both mystery fans and "seekers after unconventional story-telling" will find "tart and original pleasures" in this novel.

STONES

D139 Garebian, Keith. "Findley's Fine Line Between Untidy Life and Orderly Art." *Quill & Quire*, Nov. 1988, p. 17.

The stories in *Stones* are defined by many elements: a theatricality in imagery and characterization, an evocative sense of Toronto, a compassion for "emotional desperadoes," and an urge for retrospective regeneration. Garebian describes the two pairs of complementary stories in the collection. In "Bragg and Minna" and "A Gift of Mercy," Findley explores the tormented relationship between a husband and wife.

Although Garebian finds that in these stories ". . . the sense of place is thrillingly effective, as is the sense of drama," he feels they would have been even better if they had been combined into a novella. In the other pair, "The Name's the Same" and "Real Life Writes Real Bad," Findley "glides in and out of the past" to explore the chasm between two brothers. Some of the other stories in the collection are "melodramatic, more contrived than credible." "Stones" is the best story; it attempts to "avoid sentimentality in the re-creation of a troubled political period and an anguished family history."

D140 Mackay, Gillian. "The Naked City: Timothy Findley Goes Home to Toronto." *Maclean's*, 14 Nov. 1988, pp. 64-65.
Findley has set his novels in diverse and far-away locations but, in the stories in *Stones*, he has "returned to his own backyard to explore a world topographically greyer but no less absorbing than the more exotic locales he has favored in the past." The cultural metaphor for Findley's Toronto is the Queen Street Mental Health Centre; his characters are "dream walkers treading dangerously close to madness." In these "engrossing, exquisitely observed stories," Findley attacks the comfortable certainties of modern urban life.

D141 Adachi, Ken. "Nothing Is Left Vague in Findley's Baroque Stories." *The Toronto Star*, 19 Nov. 1988, p. M5.
While *Stones* is "an unremittingly bleak book," it is also "far from being merely depressing in effect." This is because Findley has "an extraordinary gift for inventing small significant incidents, for entering into other people's personalities and plights, and allowing the reader to see what is both crazy and recognizable . . . ." In several stories Findley fuses reality and illusion to create a "world of arrested movement and decayed memory." The stories are closer to poetry in their attention to language and form, and Adachi singles out the title story, "Stones," for special praise.

D142 Bissoondath, Neil. "The Illusion of a Spinner of Tales." *The Globe and Mail* [Toronto], 19 Nov. 1988, "Books: Literary Supplement," p. E5.
The stories in this collection are, "in a word, wonderful." Findley tells his "discomforting tales of mental anguish in a spare but mesmerizing language." His characters are "complex, fully realized individuals." The Queen Street Mental Health Centre is an ongoing motif that informs

even the few stories in which it is not mentioned. The act of scattering ashes in the first and last stories creates a "satisfying circle." Findley is "a writer of prodigious talents who, through an uncalculated modesty, maintains the illusion that he is a simple spinner of tales."

D143   Schieder, Rupert. "The Overthrow of Silence." *Books in Canada,* Dec. 1988, pp. 22-23.

Stones is not just a collection of nine separate stories, but consists of nine narratives that are "inextricably joined or linked, in various ways." Some of these links are between characters; some are linked to other Findley works. Their thematic consistency makes the stories "a unified, self-contained work and at the same time part of the larger unity of Findley's fictional world." These "latest bulletins from the world of Timothy Findley" are disturbing, an effect intensified by the realistic solidity of his characters' physical world. Findley succeeds in making these characters "quite acceptable, almost ordinary." This success is due to the structure, which is "often a relentless process of unfolding and revelation," and to Findley's "adroit handling of point of view or angle of narration." A homosexual writer is given a central role in *Stones* and Bragg is one of the few characters who achieves a final positive resolution. The collection is "one of Findley's most disturbing and at the same time, finest works."

D144   Pollock, Julie. "Findley Examines Urban Life Finds a Cold, Bleak Situation." *The Gazette* [Univ. of Western Ontario], 6 Dec. 1988, p. 24.

The stories in *Stones* contain insight into the problems of modern urban life. Findley describes the frightening and alienating sides of life with understanding and compassion. Pollock divides the stories into three sections: the Bragg and Minna stories concern a "marriage of opposites," the next three are stories of the inexplicable, and the last four deal with tragic family situations. In these last stories, Findley demonstrates his ability to "pierce the surface of the family unit, entering the core of truth." The collection's title story is "wonderfully apt."

D145   Novak, Barbara. "Brilliant Short Stories All Touch on Madness." *London Free Press,* 10 Dec. 1988, p. D12.

Stylistically, the stories in *Stones* reflect the broad range of Findley's novels, but they are unified by theme. Each "touches in some way on madness, on the anguish of perceiving the world, or oneself, in a particularly harsh and unforgiving light." The horror of this condition is, however, mitigated by an awareness of the human capacity for love. Novak comments on the naturalism of "The Name's the Same" and "Real Life Writes Real Bad." "Stones" reaches the "zenith" of the short story form. "He achieves more in this 17–page story than he did in *The Wars*, in which he examined many of the same themes." Novak credits Findley's acting career for his superb sense of scene structure. His stories read like carefully constructed plays. Findley does not hesitate to linger on an image, and the result is "a succession of perfect moments that add up to a brilliant whole."

Selected Play Reviews

CAN YOU SEE ME YET?

D146   Fraser, John. "Significance Abounds — But It's a Mighty Bore." *The Globe and Mail* [Toronto], 2 March 1976, p. 14.
    Can You See Me Yet? is "an intensely literary play that is out stalking both symbolism and significance all night." But it is "an almighty bore . . . a play laid low by its own high endeavor." Findley seems to have succumbed to the portentiousness of the Canadian theatre. Fraser praises the actors' performances and "many small details of Findley's work."
    See C117.

D147   Galloway, Myron. "Findley Achieves Great Play with *Can You See Me Yet?*". *The Montreal Star*, 2 March 1976, p. B7.
    Can You See Me Yet? is "a great play" that is "so brilliantly executed it bears no trace of having been painstakingly manufactured." Findley seamlessly weaves together the elements of Cassandra's past and present life. The work is "so stunning" that it will take audiences and critics some time to appreciate, but it "raises the level of Canadian playwrighting, for the first time in our history, to an art."

D148   Stoneham, Gordon. "Insipid New Canadian Drama." *The Citizen* [Ottawa], 2 March 1976, p. 48.
    Stoneham finds nothing to praise in *Can You See Me Yet?* except the

professional skill of the actors. The play is "deliberately obtuse . . . lacking in dramatic impact, and . . . patently pretentious." It has "no texture, no atmosphere . . . no validity."

D149   Maskoulis, Julia. "Impassioned Play Fails to Reach Ottawa Audience." *The Gazette* [Montreal], 3 March 1976, p. 43.

Findley has written "an angry and impassioned play about man's inhumanity to man . . . ." The anger comes through, but the anguish and passion fail to reach the audience. The first half is "plodding," and the actors seem unsure of their credibility while, in the second half, the audience is more moved by the characters' traumas. "The failure of this production is in under-playing Cassandra's anguish."

JOHN A. — HIMSELF!

D150   Bale, Doug. "John A. — Himself! Potentially Fine Play." *The London Free Press*, 1 Feb. 1979, p. C5.

Findley's "musical, mythical mini-history of Canada's first prime minister" is a lot like all Canadian history — "moments of inspired achievement alternating with periods of humdrum and triviality." It is a "potentially fine play that simply needs more work."

D151   Whittaker, Herbert. "John A. the Ultimate Ham." *The Globe and Mail* [Toronto], 2 Feb. 1979, p. 12.

In his "biographical vaudeville," Findley scorns "mere historical reconstruction" to emphasize the theatrical aspects of Macdonald's life. Victorian comedy in the first act gives way to Victorian pathos in the second as Findley "piles on the tragic situations." Findley owes some inspiration to newspaper caricatures from Macdonald's time.

D152   Ashley, Audrey M. "Odd Mix of Styles Confuses Audience." *The Citizen* [Ottawa], 5 Feb. 1979, p. 27.

Timothy Findley and actor William Hutt have succeeded in "creating a living portrait" of Canada's first Prime Minister. Findley has chosen "a kind of vaudeville approach," but some of the roles are played in a "straight-faced fashion." In the second act, Findley appears to change his approach, "insisting that we take the man seriously." The conflicting styles and approaches result in a "disconcerting" experience for the audience.

Selected Television Reviews

THE PAPER PEOPLE

D153 Morris, Guy. "Paper People Plumbs Emotions." *Cinema Canada*, No. 33 (Nov.–Dec. 1967), pp. 6, 20.
The Paper People is "a fascinating film" that "won't please everyone." While at times confusing and over indulgent, it does involve the viewer in the story. Much of the dialogue, intended to sound deep and meaningful, is "embarrassingly trite and meaningless." The main fault in the film is that the relationship between the artist and the filmmakers never gets beyond a superficial level.

D154 Kieran, Sheila H. "*The Paper People*: Pretentious, Sickeningly Arty — and Boring." *The Globe and Mail* [Toronto], 7 Dec. 1967, p. 14.
The Paper People is "pretentious, arty . . . and downright boring." Most of it is "insufferably arrogant . . . made by the few for the few." The CBC made the film in colour, but much of its effect is lost since only 5% of Canadian homes have colour televisions.

D155 Blackburn, Bob. Rev. of *The Paper People*. *The Telegram* [Toronto], 13 Dec. 1967, p. 37.
Although Blackburn admits he doesn't know what it is about, *The Paper People* is "exciting" television. Findley "has jumped on his hobby horse and ridden madly off in all directions." It is a "magnificent piece of television" involving total use of the medium, particularly colour.

D156 Pearce, Pat. "Paper People Cut Flimsy Figures." *The Montreal Star*, 14 Dec. 1967, p. 62.
The Paper People is "cut by writer Timothy Findley from some highly-colored but pretty flimsy cloth." The play has neither a valid cast nor a valid story.

D157 Penn, Frank. "A B-B Backfire." *The Citizen* [Ottawa], 14 Dec. 1967, p. 43.
Penn compares an advance showing of *The Paper People* in colour to its scheduled television broadcast in black-and-white and finds the latter "pretty pallid." The film-within-a-film concept is effective when emphasized by colour/black-and-white changes, but this effect is lost on non-colour televisions.

D158 Wedman, Les. Rev. of *The Paper People. The Vancouver Sun*, 14 Dec. 1967, p. 26.

The Paper People shows what Canadian television can do "when flexible and uncluttered artistic minds set out to experiment boldly." CBC's bitter-sweet production "created satisfying excitement, an air of discovery and suspense from start to finish." Findley is obviously familiar with phoneys and "high-living, low-life society." He has written scenes that "one might wish were mere figments of a fertile imagination."

D159 Dube, Bernard. "The Paper People." *The Gazette* [Montreal], 15 Dec. 1967, p. 28.

The CBC has recently undertaken some "large gambles," experimental works that fashion motion picture art out of contemporary life. *The Paper People* is one of them. The technique of having the artist's life unfold through the recollections of those who knew him is "not particularly successful." As a character, the artist does not grow in the course of the play. Dube concludes that the play "is both irritating and absorbing."

THE WHITEOAKS OF JALNA

D160 Miller, Jack. "Jalna: New TV Shines, But Late." *The Toronto Star*, 7 Jan. 1972, p. 24.

The first two episodes of *The Whiteoaks of Jalna* "differed widely in the quality of writing." The series "starts slowly and confusingly" with a complex plot and too many characters and time changes. Miller questions whether television audiences are ready for this, "in sophistication and perception."

D161 Adilman, Sid. Rev. of *The Whiteoaks of Jalna. Variety* [New York], 16 Feb. 1972, p. 47.

Adilman calls the pilot episode of *The Whiteoaks of Jalna* "a superior achievement." It "displayed a flowing panorama of filmic beauty, and Victorian sentimentality always kept in check." Findley has "infused new life into the fusty novels" of Mazo de la Roche. If future episodes are as good as the pilot, Adilman predicts "a success unmatched in previous years" for the CBC.

D162 Robertson, Heather. "Television: Jalna Is Like the Titanic, So Let's Hope It Sinks." *Maclean's*, March 1972, p. 84.
Robertson has nothing good to say about *The Whiteoaks of Jalna*. "There is little discernible plot . . . the acting is wooden, the characters flat . . . a visual and verbal cliché." This production indicates CBC's tendency to opt for "whatever is currently pop, hip or mod."

Selected Film Reviews

THE WARS

D163 Knelman, Martin. "Novel Approaches." Rev. of *The Tin Flute*, by Gabrielle Roy; and *The Wars*, by Timothy Findley. *Toronto Life*, Nov. 1983, p. 68.
Although *The Wars* is "by no means a great film, it's civilized and polished and respectable." Knelman finds it "a bit pat" and attributes its limitations to Findley's novel, which has "some great sequences and an impressively sustained ironic distance to make up for its lack of emotional depth and original ideas." Director Robin Phillips captures the tone of the book; he has "framed the action effectively and given it the resonance of being filtered through time and memory."

D164 Anthony, George. "*The Wars*: A Winner." *The Toronto Sun*, 11 Nov. 1983, p. 101.
Anthony describes *The Wars* as a "stunning film essay of manners and morality in turn-of-the-century Canada, punctuated with some sizzling Freudian overtones." Fans of Findley's novel who have been anxiously awaiting the film version can set their minds at ease. The film is "well worth seeing by anyone who likes gripping, complex cinema served up with style."

D165 Scott, Jay. "*The Wars* on Film Bruises the Heart." *The Globe and Mail* [Toronto], 11 Nov. 1983, p. E1.
"Marinated in melancholy and steeped in psychological and political skepticism," *The Wars* begins the "exciting prospect of reclaiming the Canadian past." It is the first "Australian-Canadian" film in style and "unapologetic self-absorption." Findley's novel has lost texture in its transformation into film; the book was a kaleidoscope of complexity

and the film is an inventory of incident — "but what incident!" *The Wars* is "a historically important event."

D166 Delaney, Marshall. "Another Casualty." *Saturday Night*, Feb. 1984, pp. 73-74.

Despite an exceptionally promising combination of talent and backing, *The Wars* is "dramatically hollow, cinematically inept, and psychologically unconvincing." Findley, "confident in his own sense of the characters," failed to produce a script that involves the audience in their actions. The film is a series of "unconnected and emotionally meaningless incidents."

INDEX TO CRITICS LISTED IN THE BIBLIOGRAPHY